The WRITER'S *little* HELPER

Everything you need to know
to write better and get published

W

WRITER'S DIGEST BOOKS
www.writersdigest.com

James V. Smith, Jr.

Visit our Web site at www.writersdigest.com for information on more resources for writers.

To receive a free weekly e-mail newsletter delivering tips and updates about writing and about Writer's Digest products, register directly at our Web site at http://news letters.fwpublications.com.

10 09 08 07 06   5 4 3 2 1

Distributed in Canada by Fraser Direct
100 Armstrong Avenue
Georgetown, ON, Canada L7G 5S4
Tel: (905) 877-4411

Distributed in the U.K. and Europe by David & Charles
Brunel House, Newton Abbot, Devon, TQ12 4PU, England
Tel: (+44) 1626 323200, Fax: (+44) 1626 323319
E-mail: mail@davidandcharles.co.uk

Distributed in Australia by Capricorn Link
P.O. Box 704, Windsor, NSW 2756 Australia
Tel: (02) 4577-3555

Library of Congress Cataloging-in-Publication Data

Smith, James V., Jr.
  The writer's little helper : everything you need to know to write better and get published / by James V. Smith, Jr.
    p. cm.
  Includes index.

  ISBN 13: 978-158297-422-4 (hardcover : alk. paper)
  ISBN 10: 1-58297-422-5
  1. Authorship. 2. Authorship—Marketing. I. Title.
PN147.S495 2006
808'.02—dc22

                                        2005019587

Edited by Michelle Ruberg
Designed by Claudean Wheeler
Production coordinated by Robin Richie

fw

F+W PUBLICATIONS, INC.

ABOUT THE AUTHOR

James V. Smith, Jr., has published more than a dozen novels, including the six-book series, "Force Recon." His latest novels, the "Delta Force" series written under the pen name John Harriman, use the full range of the new pacing tools introduced in this little helper.

He's a former combat soldier, helicopter pilot, newspaper writer and editor, national award-winning columnist, and magazine editor. He lives in Montana with his wife, Susan.

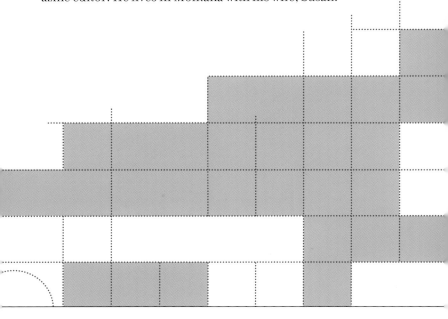

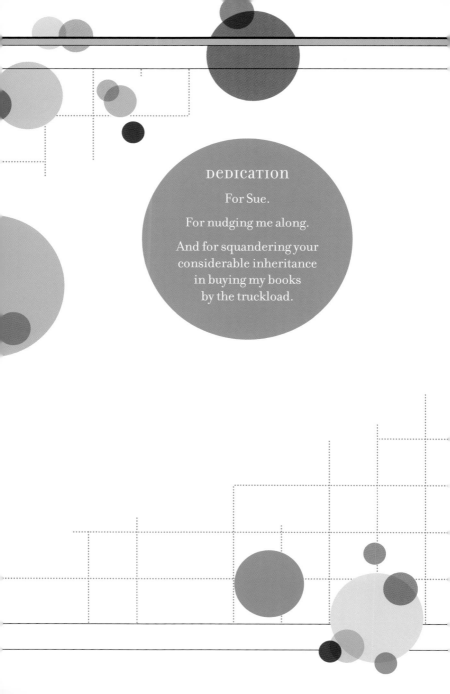

DEDICATION

For Sue.

For nudging me along.

And for squandering your considerable inheritance in buying my books by the truckload.

ACKNOWLEDGMENTS

Sometimes you need a lot more than ideas and talent. Sometimes you simply must get lucky. As I have been in sliding down the chute and landing in the midst of earnest, friendly professionals.

At Writer's Digest

Thank you, Jane Friedman, for calling me back from the brink of disaster. How did you know? And how did you have just the right words of inspiration?

Thank you, Michelle Ruberg, for your insights and instincts in handling the output with such grace under pressure. Where do you get the patience?

Thank you, Claudean Wheeler, for your way cool design. Where do you get these wild ideas? And speaking of wild ideas …

At the Peter Rubie Literary Agency

Thank you, Peter Rubie, for calling at just the moment I was struck with a wild idea. Or was it you who had the wild idea? No matter. Thank you.

TABLE *of* CONTENTS

TABLE OF CONTENTS

TABLE OF CONTENTS

GETTING
started

WHAT WILL THIS LITTLE HELPER DO FOR YOU?

☐ **Inspire you.** Of course, I'll try to do that. Any book like this first has to give you a feeling of, "I can write and sell a novel. I want to do it. I will do it—outta my way." I've tried to inspire you.

☐ **Answer your technical questions.** You want to know how to write characters that compel. You have questions about plots, setting, style, story, structure, and dialogue. Good topics all, and we'll address them, but not as other how-to books do. Where this book differs is in its point of view:

> *This book hits the technical aspects of writing fiction from the point of view of giving readers what they want in a best-seller.*

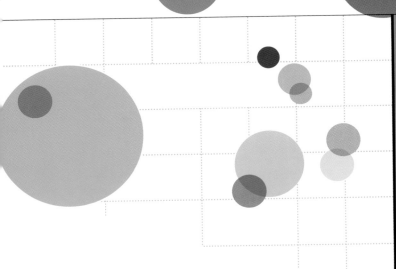

- **Give you tools.** Most writing how-tos use checklists, short-cuts, exercises, and steps—tools you can use to write fiction. This book does, too. But again, with that unique twist. While other books tell you what a writer must do—from a writer's point of view—this one comes at the writer from the angle of what readers say they want a writer to do.

- **Inject your fiction with a touch of magic.** Admit it. You want a book like this to guarantee you a best-seller. This book will simply tell you how to analyze the needs of readers and show you how best-selling writers meet those needs.

Whether you write the best-seller depends on the magic in your fiction.

CHARACTERS,
characters,
CHARACTERS

WHAT'S THE MOST IMPORTANT KEY TRAIT OF BEST-SELLING AUTHORS?

If you take only one key trait from best-selling authors, this is the one.

A writer becomes a best-seller when she learns to connect on a personal level with millions of readers. In one way or another, she satisfies a need in the heart and soul of most every person. She connects on an I-to-me level in her stories, her words, her lyrical rhythms, her characters. This, if you drew it, would look like an enormous web of connections, millions of single strands, each strand leading from each reader's soul to the writing and, ultimately, to the writer's soul. Not every best-seller is well written. But every best-seller has this mystical, if not magical, power to connect with readers on a personal, intimate level.

THE KEY CONNECTION: CHARACTERS

Except for a few best-selling authors whose action and plot ideas are killer, action and plot ideas don't count for much if the characters are cardboard cutouts. No amount of special effects can rescue a film tale with boring characters.

Peter Rubie wrote in *The Elements of Storytelling* (Wiley Books for Writers), "The story is not about what happens, but the character to whom it happens."

Peter and I are of like minds. When I taught journalism, I hammered on this point: News is what happens to people.

Now that I write and coach writers, I have a new but similar point to hammer into heads:

Story is what happens to people.

Before you begin writing, ask yourself: Does my idea for the next great American novel lend itself to telling a story about what happens to people?

a Brief writer's self-examination

List three memorable pieces of fiction: the works you most admire, the books, plays, or films you wish you'd written.

Now be honest with yourself. It's the characters, isn't it? They're the reason you admire those works, right?

Create memorable characters and you'll be well on the way to writing memorable fiction that future writers will list when they take this self-exam.

ORGANIZING
ten
EASY SCENES

Should you outline? Nah. Don't bother. Outlining systems become missions in themselves without adding to the creative aspects of writing. Here's a device that's so much simpler.

THE Ten-scene TOOL

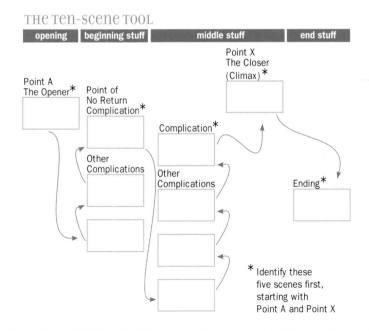

Use this tool to sketch in the ten most important scenes in your novel. No subplots, no detours, no kidding. For your central plot or main story line, these ten scenes will carry the freight. You'll choose your most dramatic, most telling, most compelling points in the story. Everything else having to do with a main story line involves creating other devices that provide characterization, motivation, minor scenes, and other fiction tools for carrying a reader's interest and involvement between the ten most important scenes.

Every novel I've ever written, ever read, or ever heard about can be destructured into ten scenes. The same goes for plays, films, and teleplays.

Notice, I'm not suggesting that the creators of these works of fiction used only ten scenes to tell the story. I'm just saying you should plan the central story line of your novel to go ten scenes or fewer. I'm arguing that if you write the central story well in these ten scenes, the rest of the novel will take care of itself.

The tool helps you to simplify. When you're finished writing the scene headlines in the boxes, you will have a central story line intact. Adjust it as your novel progresses, adding or amending as new developments occur to you. When you get stumped in the middle of your novel, refer back to these ten scenes to remind yourself where you're supposed to be going. In other words, adhere to this fundamental ...

RULE OF THUMB: Stick to the central story line by using the Ten-Scene Tool and you will avoid most fatal structural mistakes made by amateur fiction writers.

You will avoid:

- Excess story complexity, over-plotting
- Wandering
- Over-writing
- Inability to explain what the story's about
- And a host of other sins.

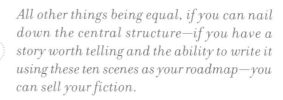

> *All other things being equal, if you can nail down the central structure—if you have a story worth telling and the ability to write it using these ten scenes as your roadmap—you can sell your fiction.*

To make it easier, I've cut your job in half to get your started. Just sketch in the headlines of the five scenes with asterisks in them.

Then pick one scene. Begin writing there. When you're satisfied that you have set down the essence of that scene, start with another. When you have five done, write five more.

After that, you don't need a stinking tool. You'll know what to do next.

Happy writing.

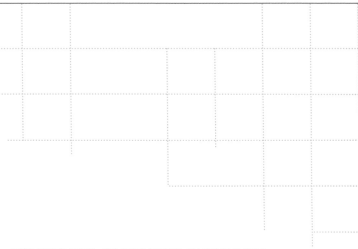

try the ten-scene tool right now

Pick a story of your own. You know the one.

It might be that idea you've been noodling in your head for months or even years. Go ahead. Commit it to paper. Put down the headlines for your Opener. Your Closer. Fill in the rest of the blank boxes. Or …

It might be the great Chapter One you can't get past. Plug it into the tool. What comes next? What comes after that? Or …

It might be the two hundred pages in a dusty corner of your closet. Pull it out. Extract the big scenes and reduce them to headlines in the Ten-Scene Tool.

Take it from there. You know what to do. Congratulations. You're on the way to getting done with your story.

THE
twenty-one
KEY
TRAITS

WHAT DO READERS WANT?

Readers want to read works that offer utility (writing to the point, about things they can use in their lives). They seek information, substance, focus, logic, a sense of connection, a compelling style, a sense of wit, simplicity, clarity, a fast pace, imagery, creativity, excitement, comfort, happiness, and truth (if not truth, then fact or at least balance and fairness). They seek writing that provokes them. They want active, memorable writing. They want to say, "Wow!" at writing that leaves them with a sense of wonder. They honor writing that elevates them with its transcendence (heroism, justice, beauty, honor, honesty, and the like).

THE 21 KEY TRAITS OF BEST-SELLING FICTION

☐ **Utility** (writing about things that people will use in their lives)

☐ **Information** (facts people must have to place your writing in context)

☐ **Substance** (the relative value or weight in any piece of writing)

☐ **Focus** (the power to bring an issue into clear view)

☐ **Logic** (a coherent system for making your points)

☐ **A sense of connection** (the stupid power of personal involvement)

☐ **A compelling style** (writing in a way that engages)

☐ **A sense of humor** (wit or at least irony)

☐ **Simplicity** (clarity and focus on a single idea)

☐ **Entertainment** (the power to get people to enjoy what you write)

☐ **A fast pace** (the ability to make your writing feel like a quick read)

☐ **Imagery** (the power to create pictures with words)

☐ **Creativity** (the ability to invent)

☐ **Excitement** (writing with energy that infects a reader with your own enthusiasm)

☐ **Comfort** (writing that imparts a sense of well-being)

☐ **Happiness** (writing that gives joy)

☐ **Truth** (or at least fairness)

☐ **Writing that provokes** (writing to make people think or act)

☐ **Active, memorable writing** (the poetry in your prose)

☐ **A sense of *Wow!*** (the wonder your writing imparts on a reader)

☐ **Transcendence** (writing that elevates with its heroism, justice, beauty, honor)

The checklist, my friend, is the essence of compelling fiction. To quote Stern from *Schindler's List*, to a writer, "The list is life."

To sell your fiction, you must pay attention to the Key Traits of Best-Selling Fiction.

FYI, the twenty-one traits are arranged in a kind of rough order.

☐ **Appeals to the intellect.** The first five: *utility* to *logic*. To you, the writer, they refer to how you research, organize, and structure your story. These are the large-scale mechanics of a novel.

☐ **Appeals to the emotions.** From a *sense of connection* to *excitement*. These are the ways you engage a reader to create buzz. Do these things right, and people will talk about your novel, selling it to others.

☐ **Appeals to the soul.** *Comfort* through *transcendence*. With these traits you examine whether your writing matters, whether it lasts, whether it elevates you to the next level as a novelist.

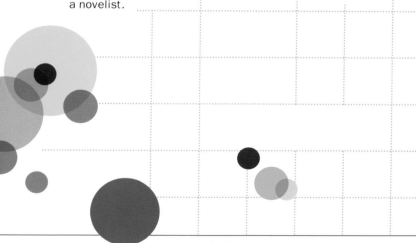

where do the 21 key traits come from?

They come from the most prolific, most complete, most accessible, most reliable survey of book readers in the world. They come from my study of the thousands of reader reviews on Amazon.com.

Reliable? Yes. Why? Because most reviewers visit a page to write reviews based on their emotional reactions to books. They either love a book or hate it. They were either swept away by the characters and story and language. Or they felt cheated by the author. Either way, they have to speak out.

You can duplicate my research. I analyzed reviews of bestsellers, the good reviews, the bad, and the ugly. I found patterns in the way people responded and sorted reader remarks into categories.

Go ahead. Find the best-selling book in the area where you want to write fiction. Find your own patterns in the first two hundred reviews. I'd be astonished if they were far from my list. These are readers telling writers what they want—or in the instance of a bad review, what they don't want. You can learn a ton from this kind of market survey. Give it a go.

Then get to writing to satisfy your readers.

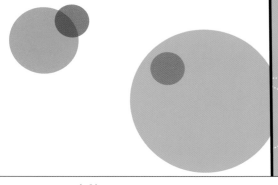

THE
passive
VOICE
DEFINED

WHAT IS THE PASSIVE VOICE?

Good question. Here's a short primer on the passive voice.

Sorry to say, passive voice is a grammar term. But we must look into it. First, it's a major factor in reading ease. And second, amateur writers abuse the passive voice terribly and often. Probably because it's a mainstay of the business world.

Corporate writers tend to use passive voice to excess, often to a level of 40 percent or higher. The passive sucks the life out of writing. So be aware when you use it.

Clearly, any writer who uses the passive in 40 percent of his sentences isn't aware of it. Right? That's why we need to define the term.

Remember the dreaded diagram from school?

SUBJECT | VERB | OBJECT

In this simple diagram of the active voice, the subject of the sentence goes ahead of the verb, or action word. The object of the sentence receives the action.

But let's get away from abstract terms. Here's an actual sentence, ripped from the headlines, in the active voice:

Rhonda eats the alien.

The subject of the sentence, *Rhonda*, acts, that is, she's the eater. The verb is *eats*. Not just to throw around grammar terms, but *alien* is the object, the direct object of the action acted out by the actor. Or if you like, the alien is the eatee. Diagram it, and you get ...

RHONDA | EATS | ALIEN

To put this crime against nature into the passive voice is simple. The subject of the sentence is acted upon. As in ...

The alien is eaten by Rhonda.

What happened here?

Rhonda is still the eater. *Is eaten* becomes the action, a change from the simpler *eats*. *Alien* is still the eatee.

But since the eatee now goes before the verb, and the eater goes after, this is the passive voice.

Is passive voice a bad thing? No. Of course not. Let's put a reality on the table: Using passive voice is not a crime. The passive sentence is a perfectly legit writing tool. But the passive does have its downside, too.

THE PITFALLS OF PASSIVE VOICE

Passive voice uses more words than active voice to express the same idea. Rhonda eats the alien grew from four words to six. Big deal, you say. In fact, it is a big deal. That's a 50 percent increase in the number of words—in one sentence.

Passive voice also softens the impact of writing. You won't want to do that in tense action scenes.

Passive voice is sometimes harder to read and more difficult to understand. And not just because it uses more words. In long sentences, you often have to reread parts to find the bottom line or to search for the actor, if one even exists, because it's at the tail end.

So. That's the passive. Here's a quick review of passive voice and a brief exercise.

BOTTOM LINE: Unless you are using the passive with purpose, that is, to mellow out a passage, to avoid giving away a clue, or to slow down the pace of your novel, don't use it. Like most writing coaches, I urge you to use the active voice most of the time.

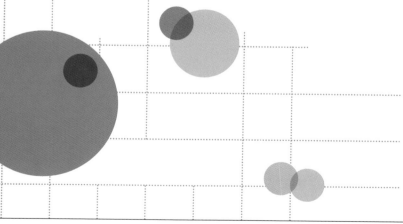

a BIT OF a passive exercise

Write these sentences into the active voice:

> The battle was begun by the scouts blundering into each other in the night. But the war—the war was begun by politicians blundering in the light.

_____
_____
_____

> She was swept up in her own emotions, carried away by daydreams, buried in fantasy.

_____
_____
_____

> He was struck twice, first by fear, then by the realization that he loved her.

_____
_____
_____

Now go back and re-evaluate each of your changes. Do you find that at least one or two of the sample sentences read better in the passive, maybe even all three? Good. The point of this exercise is to assure you that the passive is not always a bad thing. Don't let any writing how-to book tell you otherwise.

IMAGERY
versus
DESCRIPTION

My advice: Never write description. Description implies stopping the story to write colorful stuff. Instead, create powerful imagery. Which suggests keeping the story in motion using those images to pump up the action, conflict, and dialogue.

CHECKLIST FOR CREATING POWERFUL IMAGERY

☐ **Paint the image in small bites.** Never stop your story to describe. Keep it going, incorporating vivid images, enlarging the action, and putting the dialogue in context.

> A sponge carpet of pine needles covered the trail. It cushioned their soles and absorbed the sounds of their footsteps.
>
> Rhonda stopped short and whispered, "Something's coming. There. To the right. A bear?"

☐ **Incorporate images into action.** Suppose I had written:

> A million years of discarded pine needles lay on the forest floor, carpeting the trail.

That's description. Static. The author's talking. Can you hear him reading from an encyclopedia? The difference in the first version is tying their walking to soundless footsteps. This clears the way for Rhonda to hear and see.

> She pointed at a looming hulk, for all the good that pointing would do in the ink of night.
> "Bill grasped her arm. "No. It couldn't be."
> But the crashing of brush told them it could.
> "Yes. Get up a tree."

☐ **See through the character's eyes.** Hear through her ears. When you can, use the character's senses instead of the author's. It's called character point of view.

> She felt her pulse both in her throat and under the grip of that hand of his crushing her forearm. His breath. She heard it in short, chattering bursts. She smelled it, too. Fear stunk.

☐ **Use the tiny but telling detail.**

> She tore free of his grip and leaped off the trail. A spider's web tugged at her face. Any other time she would have screamed. She ran into a tree, a rough pine bough slapped her breasts, and needles stabbed at her eyes. Any other time she would have cursed.

The spider's web. Ever ran into one?

❑ **Choose action-bearing verbs.** *Cushioned, absorbed, stopped, whispered, pointed, grasped, tore, leaped, tugged, screamed, ran, slapped, stabbed, cursed.* These words do so much more than say what is. They indicate first fear, then panic.

❑ **Choose action-bearing non-verbs.** *Looming* is a verb form used as an adjective. *Crashing* is used as a noun.

❑ **Invent fresh viewpoints.**

> She climbed blindly. And so quickly. Like a ladder. That was scary. If she could scale this pine so easily, couldn't the bear climb it, too?
>
> She drove her head into a branch. But the sound of crying wasn't hers.
>
> "Help. It's got me."
>
> Bill. Oh, God, Bill.
>
> The bear had him. Still she climbed, seeing nothing but sparklers of pain in her head.
>
> He shrieked at her from the dark below.
>
> She did not—could not—respond.

This is the viewpoint of a woman in panic and pain. When she looks into the darkness, she sees only sparklers. Clearly, she's so frightened, she's only trying to save herself.

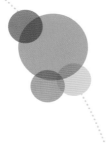

❏ Create an image without saying so.

> The pine limbs now bent like those of a Christmas tree.
> A fresh breeze chilled her skin.
>
> "Bill," she whispered. "Speak to me, for God's sake,
> speak to me, Bill."
>
> But he did not. All she could hear was snorting and
> thrashing. She put a hand to her mouth. She thought she
> might scream but nothing came out of her mouth. Fear
> of attracting the bear kept her quiet. The pitch on her
> hand glued her lips shut.
>
> And, yes, the shame. That silenced her, too.

The thin limbs bending and the fresh breeze tells us Rhonda
has climbed high into the tree. The chill tells us she's been
sweating. And the pitch, though she and we didn't notice it
in the climbing, is there on her hands and face.

minimum
CHARACTER
ELEMENTS
FOR ANY
STORY

Does my story have ...

A TRULY HEROIC CHARACTER?
AND IS THAT CHARACTER ...

❏ Distinctive in voice and attitude?

❏ Likable, even if quirky?

❏ Interesting in career or skills?

❏ Honorable, even if not saintly?

❏ Flawed or vulnerable, either physically or emotionally?

❏ Able to connect with readers in matters of the human condition?

❏ Capable of humor or irony?

- [ ] Capable of fear but not enduring cowardice?
- [ ] Physically appealing but not a perfect ten?
- [ ] Alive at the end of the story?

A HEROIC CHARACTER'S WORTHY GOAL QUEST? AND IS THAT GOAL OR QUEST ...

- [ ] Substantial in content?
- [ ] Difficult to attain?
- [ ] Generally legal and honorable?
- [ ] Shared by potential readers?
- [ ] Contested by any number of forces? Especially ...

THE HEROIC CHARACTER'S WORTHY ADVERSARY? AND IS THAT ADVERSARY ...

- [ ] Distinctive in voice or attitude?
- [ ] Continually in competition with the heroic character?
- [ ] Likable or sympathetic to some extent?
- [ ] Interesting in career, crimes, or skills?
- [ ] Wicked but not entirely demonic?
- [ ] Flawed or vulnerable, either physically, mentally, or emotionally?
- [ ] Capable of humor or irony?
- [ ] Powerful enough to crush the heroic character?
- [ ] Physically fascinating, even if repulsive?
- [ ] Defeated at the end of the story?

**ACTION AND CONFLICT INVOLVING
THE HEROIC CHARACTER'S QUEST? WITH ...**

☐ Suspense or substantial tension at every turn?

☐ All dialogue laced with conflict?

☐ A varied pace?

☐ Action either rising to a confrontation or falling from one?

☐ Utter absence of boring, static scenes?

☐ Vivid imagery rather than lifeless description?

☐ Singularity of the central story line?

☐ Subplots that support the central story line?

☐ Narration carried by characters and not the author?

☐ Absence of philosophizing, preaching, and musing?

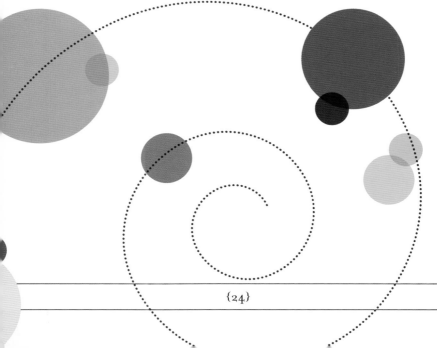

- ☐ A final, titanic, climactic struggle between characters at story's end?
- ☐ The climax being the most powerful scene in the story?
- ☐ A resolution that offers redemption to the heroic character?
- ☐ Recognition that every element in the story pointed to the end?
- ☐ Lessons learned, for both characters and readers?

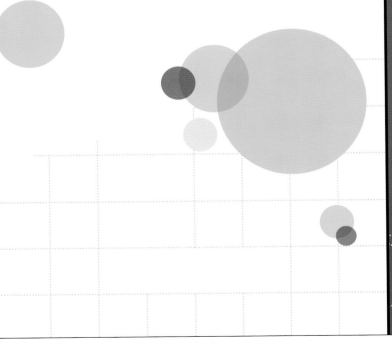

CHARACTER

AVOIDING
amateur
MISTAKES

First and foremost: STAY OUT OF THE STORY.

Don't stick your nose into the fictional world with expressions like: *If she only knew what was waiting for her on the other side of that door*; and *he was wrong*; or *little did she know*.

But you probably consider these examples so elementary that it's an insult to your intelligence for me to list them. And besides, an entire *Unfortunate Events* series is hugely successful right now using that very technique. Even so. Odds are, there's really no room for you in the story.

So let me give you some of the less obvious ways an author can intrude, ways you should avoid.

INTRUSION MISTAKES TO AVOID

☐ **Tired expressions.** Like right out of sitcoms, movies, or even the day's news. Using them is like putting a stick-on note in the margin of your manuscript: *Hi, I'm the author, and I watch too much TV. Hell-OH-o, don't go there, I don't think so* as in any sitcom or teen conversation.

Goofy gimmicks and grammatical gadgets!!! Such as alliteration—writing with words that begin with the same letter—and odd punctuation like multiple exclamation points.

Cute quote marks. *She had never met an author so tall— seven feet, an authentic "literary giant."* Do you see the quotes? That's the author. He's winking at you from behind the narrative, telling you he's made a funny, wanting you to notice it. Take off the quotes, and the irony works just as well.

Preaching from the mouth of a character. When I hear a novel's heroine use a tired expression like, "male chauvinist pig," whether the language comes in quotes or not, I know the writer couldn't find a more artful, less preachy way to say the same thing.

Brand name revelations. I like concrete detail, research, and accuracy in the things I read as well as the next reader. But after the tenth new vintage wine is described, dated, and delivered, it's clear to me that the author is showing off his inner oenophile.

Politically correct assumptions and observations. Not that some characters shouldn't be written as PC. But the author shouldn't take liberties outside of character to push a theme.

☐ **Wink-and-nod.** This often involves phrases like *of course* and *naturally*. As in this example:

> Of course, he didn't say word to influence her decision to get an abortion.

Except for the writer herself, this is a tricky situation to judge. Sometimes it's a character narrator who uses the word or phrase in the sense of:

> He knew better than to try.

But it's also possible the author was speaking out.

☐ **Out-of-character narration and descriptions.** Sometimes you read words coming from a character's mouth that just don't sound familiar, a change of voice or attitude with no apparent reason for the change. That's the author showing off his big vocabulary or big-whoop opinions. I'd like to have a dime for every time I've committed this sin.

☐ **Naked clichés.** When a writer uses them stale out of the box, he's annoying his reader just as surely as chewing gum with his mouth open. The reader is thinking: *Can't this guy come up with language a bit more inventive?* Thus, the author intrusion.

☐ **Awkward constructions.** Anytime a reader stumbles over your words, you have broken through the façade of fiction to announce your presence behind the page.

- **Static situations and lengthy descriptions.** What Elmore Leonard calls the stuff readers skip. When readers skip, the writer has allowed his presence to be felt. Unpleasantly so.

- **Pontificating.** This includes philosophizing, musing, wondering, and other subtle forms of pontificating.

- **Repetition.** When you repeat a pet phrase or even an odd word in a story, it calls attention to itself. When you use it more often, it calls attention to the author. As in: *Don't you own a thesaurus?* My wife hates it when I use the phrase *state of the art,* even once.

- **Anything too, too quirky.** I like quirky writing, other writers' quirks and my own. But sometimes they can destroy the ambiance of a piece of writing. I hate to confess it, but I lose a lot in the reading of Chaucer when it's written in the original Middle English:

> Thing that is seyd is seyd; and forth it gooth.

You can forgive Chaucer those quirks because it was his English before we made it ours. But there's a line in Tom Wolfe's *Bonfire of the Vanities:*

> *Heh-hegggggggggggggggggghhhhhhhhhhhhhhhhh!*

which is an odd cackling laugh set in type. That kind of quirk could get old fast. Like the handheld camera technique in some films, especially when the cameral circles an actor half a dozen times at high speed.

When should an author's voice be heard? Never. Keep yourself out of the story altogether unless you're writing one of those fictional first-person memoirs or whatever they call them.

STRUCTURING
YOUR *first* WORDS

Most writers find the Opener the easiest scene to write. They get bit by the bug and they knock out the first three chapters in a week. And then nothing.

The hard copy of those fiery first chapters collects dust for years because the writer didn't see where the story was headed, the characters didn't take over the story as she expected, and the writing bug vanished into the humdrum of life.

My advice is to write the climax of the novel first. Even if only in sketch form. The moment you do, you have a destination. Even if only 1,000 words. From the time you sketch out that climax, you'll spend every spare moment trying to find beginnings and middles to get you to that ending material.

Even if you do write the Closer first, you'll eventually have to get to the Opener. So let's discuss its essentials.

POINT A, THE OPENER

A great opener might include any or all of the following:

❏ A great first line

❏ Excitement: high action, high drama, high anxiety

❏ An intro to the heroic character

❏ An intro to the worthy adversary

❏ Problems that stand in the way of the heroic character achieving a worthy goal

- Your best writing style, to set the tone and to show you can write: action, conflict, imagery, dialogue, irony
- A feel for the story's setting and atmosphere
- Foreshadowing of things to come
- Above all, a single overwhelming central problem that will only get worse until it appears incapable of being solved, a problem that will defeat the heroic character unless she defeats it in the Closer

How many scenes in the Opener? As many as you require to continue the momentum of the novel's first scene. Introduce characters, commit the heroic character to her worthy goal, and put the central conflict in motion, leading to the …

Point-of-no-return complication. A scene to end the Opener, the first major turning point in your novel. At the end of this PONRC scene, the writer's setup for the story is done. The reader understands the problems facing the main characters and feels certain that events have been set in motion toward some kind of inevitable, climactic confrontation. An example might demonstrate better than an academic dissertation:

In the film *Fargo*, the crank scheme at the center of the story might be undone at any time—until a state trooper and two witnesses are murdered on the road. After that point, there's no going back to the way things were for anybody in the story.

Now that's a point of no return for you.

REJECTION
ain't FATAL

IF MY MANUSCRIPT IS REJECTED, DOES THAT MEAN THE EDITOR HATES MY WORK?

Hardly. Publishing professionals often reject a work even when they don't dislike it. Take a look at the following list, not based on scientific study, which I invented to illustrate my point:

Reasons for rejection

An editor or agent might have one or a dozen reasons for rejecting your query. Here are a few.

- She hates it. Your style, your approach, your story. And you.

- She hates your topic, although she might like your writing.

- She likes your writing potential, but it'd take too much work to develop it to salable standards.

- She's never even looked at your stuff. After six months, it's time to clean out the office and send back everything with an SASE and trash everything else.

- She loves your writing, but she never takes on fiction.

- She loves your fiction, but never deals in romances.

- She loves your romance, but already has an author engaged in an identical project.
- She loves your project, but your topic went out of vogue two years ago—try again two years hence, when it makes a comeback.
- She's in the middle of a failed relationship and hasn't liked anything for months.
- She's got you confused with somebody she hates.

> *And the point I wish to illustrate? Hey, sometimes you get rejected for reasons neither you nor anybody in the business can understand. Do your best and keep on submitting until somebody learns to love your work.*

Write the first 1,000 words to compel a publishing professional to fall in love with your work. Those first four or five manuscript pages must compel an agent to forget about the ten to fifty clients he represents. They must divert him from any book deal now in progress unless it is six figures or more.

They must compel an editor to ignore the dozen or two projects she is now shepherding anywhere from acquisition to second printing. She must forget about any author she edits with a status less than that of Stephen King.

Your first 1,000 words, for at least the five minutes it takes to read them, must occupy the world of the publishing professional so completely that an editor or agent actually visualizes high six-figure deals and Stephen King status for the writer of those words.

FLASHBACKS

SHOULD I USE FLASHBACKS
TO WRITE BACKGROUND TO MY NOVEL?

Avoid them at all costs until you get famous.

Everybody knows about the flashback. Moviegoers see them all the time, usually brief scenes of a past event that help explain the motivation for a current event in the film.

Novelists write them all the time, often in a distinctive typeface or format, like italics. Most often a character will tip off the flashback by remembering the previous event. Then the event is played out. Sometimes without explanation or preamble, a scene appears, plays out, and the story resumes where it left off. Even these rough cuts or transitionless jumps usually don't bother readers or viewers.

If there's any problem with flashbacks, it is that they have become something of a cliché in fiction. Writers use them because they can so easily explain things. The trouble is, any form of explanation stops the story, whether exposition, narration, or pseudo-action played out in the trappings of the dreaded dream sequence.

TIP: All writers great and small use flashbacks. But the really talented writers use them as only one tool in an entire tool kit of transitional and texturizing devices. Lazy writers drop a flashback into the story because they don't have the energy or imagination to find some more creative method.

So I give you this brief checklist to refer to anytime you're considering writing a flashback:

- ❏ Don't. Find another, more artful technique.
- ❏ If you must resort to flashbacks, ration them. Use them sparingly, and never in the climax.
- ❏ Be brief. Illustrate your point, and get back to the story in the present.

FICTION TECHNIQUES

WHAT are my BEST CHOICES IN USING a POINT OF VIEW IN MY NOVEL?

FIRST PErSON

The I, we, me, my, mine, us narrator, often using the voice of the heroic character or a constant companion of the heroic character.

> There I was, minding my own beeswax when she up and kissed me. I near passed out.

ADVANTAGES OF THIS POINT OF VIEW

❏ It feels natural to most writers because we live in an *I*-world.

❏ You only have to deal with one mind, the narrator's.

❏ You can create a distinctive internal voice.

❏ You can add an element of craft by creating a narrator who's not entirely reliable.

DISADVANTAGES OF THIS POINT OF VIEW

❏ You can only write about what the narrator can see or sense.

❏ The narrator must constantly be on stage or observing the stage.

❏ You can't go into the minds of other characters.

SECOND PERSON

The you narrator. Rarely successful, and then only in shorter books. Check out Jay McInerney's *Bright Lights, Big City*. Most publishing experts advise against this point of view.

> You're just standing there. She comes along and kisses you, and you nearly faint.

ADVANTAGES OF THIS POINT OF VIEW

❏ You have the power to be different, even eccentric in the way you can speak to the reader so informally.

DISADVANTAGES OF THIS POINT OF VIEW

❏ It begins to feel quirky, whether you're reading it or writing it.

❏ It says to the publishing professional: *I'm a Jay McInerney knockoff. Reject me!*

THIRD PERSON

The he, she, it, they, them narrator. This point of view appears more often than any other in mainstream and category fiction. It offers you a variety of possibilities for limiting omniscience, or information that the narrator and reader is privy to in the telling of the story.

Third Person Unlimited Omniscience

The author enters the mind of any character. He transports readers to any setting or action he likes.

> He stood stiff as a fence post, watching her come his way. *What did she want?* he wondered.
>
> She had decided to kiss him, no matter what. So she did. She could see the effect of her kiss at once. He nearly fell over.

ADVANTAGES OF THIS POINT OF VIEW

❏ Different points of view offer you more chances to enrich your novel with contrasting characters the reader can identify with in turn.

❏ It allows you and your reader a breath of fresh air as you change viewpoint characters.

❏ You can broaden your novel's scope as you move from widely separated settings and conflicting points of view.

DISADVANTAGES OF THIS POINT OF VIEW

❏ You can confuse yourself and the reader unless every voice and point of view is distinctive.

❏ You can diffuse the flow and impact of your story by switching to too many points of view—notice how the last two sentences about the kiss jolt you from one observer's mind to the other.

❏ It's too easy for you to get lazy and begin narrating as the author instead of one of your characters.

Third Person Limited Omniscience

The author enters the mind of a limited number of characters.

> He stood stiff as a fence post, watching her come his way.
> *What did she want?* he wondered, as she approached. Then
> he saw the determination in her face. Good crackers!
> She was going to kiss him, no matter what.
>> She did, too, and he nearly fell over.

ADVANTAGES OF THIS POINT OF VIEW

❑ This has all the advantages of the previous point of view, plus …

❑ The ability to concentrate the story by keeping to major characters' and strategic minor characters' thoughts.

DISADVANTAGES OF THIS POINT OF VIEW

❑ There are none, really, because by imposing discipline on your points of view, you minimize all the disadvantages of unlimited omniscience.

Some writing manuals describe three or four times as many point-of-view choices. Don't analyze the topic to death. Choose one and get busy writing.

EDITING HIP SHOTS *and* QUICK TIPS

Before you send your manuscript or writing sample to an agent or editor, check for these items.

AMATEUR AND COMMON MISTAKES

☐ Avoid multiple exclamation points!!!!! Avoid even single exclamation points! Except for the case of a true exclamation, like the rare *Rats!* Or the too-rare *Cubs win!*

☐ DON'T WRITE TEXT IN ALL CAPS. It's too hard to read, and it's shouting in print. AND WHY SHOUT?

☐ Avoid *per,* as in *per instructions.* Other than uses like *words per sentence,* let cats *per.*

☐ Use the search function to find *-ly* words, adverbs. Check each adverb ending in *-ly* to see if it can be cut. Use stronger verbs and you won't need the help of adverbs.

☐ Search for *-ize* and *-ization* and cut those when you can.

☐ Search for *-tion* words, too, and cut them down to size.

Affect is a verb meaning *to influence. Effect* is sometimes a verb meaning *to produce,* but it's most often a noun, meaning *the result produced.*

Impact is a noun not a verb.

> Wrong: *The ten-pound report impacted him a lot.*
>
> Right: *The impact of the ten-pound report broke his ribs, his spirit, and his momentum up the career ladder.*

CHOOSE YOUR WORDS CAREFULLY

☐ Don't *entitle* songs, books, reports, or films— *title* them. *Entitle* refers to ownership. *I titled this book* The Writer's Little Helper. *I'm entitled to its copyright.*

☐ Don't *type up or print out; type* and *print* will do the job just fine, thank you.

☐ Don't use *et cetera* or *etc.*

☐ *Loan* is a noun, dang it, a noun; *lend* is the verb—always. You *lend* money. That money is a *loan.*

☐ Use *hopefully* the way you use a gun. If you don't know how to handle it, leave it alone. You wouldn't say, *Hopefully you will die.* Even when you mean, *It is hoped you will die.* You might say, *I hope you die.* Which still pales next to, *Drop dead.* If you insist on *hopefully,* try, *Hopefully, I give you this poison.*

☐ Use *fewer* with things you can count, *less than* with quantities. *He has fewer than ten fingers and less than enough sense.*

☐ *Imply* means *to suggest. Infer* means to *deduce.*

☐ *Its* is possessive. While *it's* is the contraction of it is. *Your* is possessive. *Get your gun. You're* is the contraction of *you are. You're gonna get it, you dirty rat.*

SCENE-ERY

How can I write the most effective scenes?

A scene is the basic building block of a piece of fiction, one that portrays characters in action, moving the story forward by their behaviors, words, and thoughts. The essential elements present in almost every scene are action, conflict, images, and dialogue—all unified by singular, dominant purpose.

When you write scenes, put the spotlight on characters. Let the reader see and hear them as they act and interact. Scenes carry the novel like pictures, action, and dialogue carry a film.

Scenes differ from narration, in which the author does the talking. I identify three types of scenes: Master, Major, and Minor.

Master scenes. These form the basis of the Ten-Scene Tool (on page 6). Your story's most significant events take place as Master scenes: The opening scene, the point-of-no-return complication, other pivotal complications (reversals and victories for your characters), the climax, and the ending. You're not limited to any number of Master scenes by the Ten-Scene Tool. You can write as many as you want. The Ten-Scene Tool forces you to simplify your central story line by focusing on a finite number of powerful scenes that drive the work. Use the following criteria for your Master scenes so you don't overwrite them.

- Always involve heroic characters or their adversaries in conflict. In the climax, the confrontation between heroic characters and their adversaries is mandatory.

- Always portray pivotal action in scenes.
- Always include dialogue, even if only internal monologue, the characters' thoughts as words to herself.

Major scenes. These are important but less than pivotal. They advance the story but don't portray important setbacks or major victories for the novel's central characters. Some criteria for Major scenes:

- You may include your heroic character or his worthy adversary, but secondary characters might just as well carry the scene.
- Use Major scenes to set up coming Master scenes.
- That is, always keep the story moving toward other important scenes.

Minor scenes. Don't let the name fool you. Treat Minor scenes as important. They add life to a story, even if they're only used to show minor action and small detail. Think of them as brushstrokes. They might be brief interludes that stand on their own and, like the other scenes, accomplish a purpose.

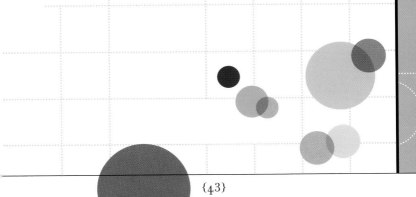

INVENTIVE
words

Successful writing means having a great story and telling it beautifully. Word choice lies at the center of beautiful story-telling. Put another way, it's hard to tell a creative story in boring words.

GETTING TO INVENTIVE WORDS

Begin with specific. Ask yourself as you write: Is this word specific enough to identify exactly what I want the reader to see as a mental image? And, if no image is needed: Does this word carry the freight without getting in the way? Example:

> The man, thin as a rail, jumped into the car as it sped away.

Fill in the blanks in this exercise. If you like a context, say the narrator of the sentence is a retired homicide detective.

CREATIVE, SPECIFIC WORD CHOICE

AUTOMATIC	LITERAL	CONCRETE	SPECIFIC	INVENTIVE
_____	man	_____	_____	_____
jumped into	_____	_____	_____	_____
_____	car	_____	_____	_____
sped away	_____	_____	_____	_____

automatic words

These are tired, first-draft words borrowed from pop culture—our TV shows, film, celebrities, politicians, and business leaders. Or teens. Ever listen to teens talk? Here, I'll do the math for you: Two kids on the phone for an hour burns no more than 100 vocabulary words, tops, with these terms used most: *I go, he goes, like, and, so not cool.* Boring.

literal

These are also first-draft quality words, the ordinary language in life's daily chit-chat. Men are big; men are small. Women are pretty; and some men are ugly, unless they're pretty ugly. Such words are useless, such words are boring. Readers yawn at them; readers stop reading them.

Literal words you might have used in the blanks above: *entered, got into, drove away, departed.*

concrete

Writing with concrete words lifts you to the plane where you begin inventing images. Not every sentence calls for poetry, but you should strive to write at all times in the world of concrete images. The instant one of your written words plants a picture in a head, you become a creative writer. Let's work with some literal and automatic words and harden them into concrete. In each case, you will see an image as well. With these words, you're getting somewhere along the path to invention. Observe.

LITTLE—the size of peppercorns

GREENISH—olive

DOG—golden retriever

WOMAN—Oprah

FOOD—sushi

BREAKFAST—eggs and bacon

APARTMENT—cold-water flat

CAR—Corvette

SPECIFIC

Use specific images to elevate your art to an even higher plane. Add character. Distinguish individuals from every other specimen within a category. Create distinctive pictures. If you can use words from this category in the draft stage it will make your revision process that much more creative. But even if you write a flat first draft, you must begin revising toward the specific in your first edit. Let's take the concrete examples and turn them into specific images.

LITTLE—the size of peppercorns—pupils the size of peppercorns

GREENISH—olive—olive drab

DOG—golden retriever—matted golden retriever

WOMAN—Oprah—Oprah without the smile

FOOD—sushi—sashimi

BREAKFAST—eggs and bacon—fried eggs and rare bacon

APARTMENT—cold-water flat—windowless cold-water flat

CAR—Corvette—Corvette convertible

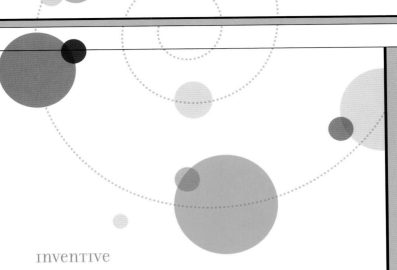

INVENTIVE

Here is where you transcend all other writing.

LITTLE—the size of peppercorns—pupils the size of peppercorns—*peppercorn eyes*

GREENISH—olive—olive drab—*olive drab dirty martini*

DOG—golden retriever—matted golden retriever—*golden retriever matted in its own drool*

WOMAN—Oprah—Oprah without the smile—*Oprah without the money*

FOOD—sushi—sashimi—*cooked sashimi*

BREAKFAST—eggs and grits—fried eggs and rare bacon—*eggs runnyside up and cold, rare bacon*

APARTMENT—cold-water flat—windowless cold-water flat—*windowless cold-water cell*

CAR—Corvette—Corvette convertible—*Corvette convertible stripped to the frame*

In each example, the final, italicized version is a precise image. That's what you shoot for. That's invention.

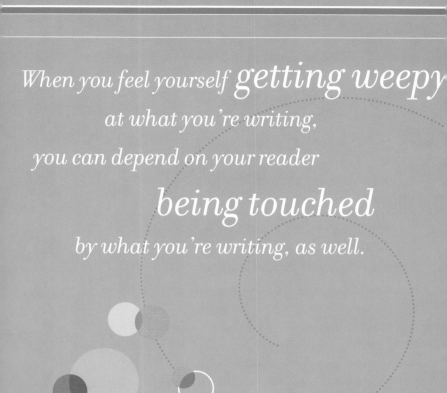

When you feel yourself *getting weepy*
at what you're writing,
you can depend on your reader

being touched

by what you're writing, as well.

When you find yourself
being amused
by what you're writing,
watch out;
you're getting too cute.

DIALOGUE

WHAT DOES GREAT DIALOGUE SOUND LIKE?

"In fiction, the characters must always get right to the point when they talk," says Dean Koontz.

If you want to learn how to write superb dialogue, study the best plays and films of our literature. If possible, study it both in performance (live or video) and in print. Read plays and screenplays to get the feel of writing on the page.

And, in the best scripts, what writing it is. Pure dialogue unadulterated by music, actor expression, pictures, or narrative transition supplied by an author. Read it aloud to get a flavor of the emotion contained within the word choices made by the writer of the screenplay. Playwrights and screenwriters who succeed at their craft are probably the best writers of dialogue you can study. By looking at such refined gold, you can learn more than from any ten books that tell you how to write dialogue.

If you want to advance your study to the graduate level, follow the steps in this little exercise.

1. Rent a video of a play or film that's best noted for its writing rather than its pretty actors and pictures. Any nominees in the Tony Awards or the screenwriting award in the Oscars will do.

2. Buy a copy of the screenplay of the film or play.

3. Decide which scenes of dialogue make the strongest impression on you. If you can't come by a copy of the screenplay, take notes as you watch the film.

4. Return to those scenes and transcribe them—if you don't have the screenplay. Print out the transcriptions so you have a hard copy in hand for the next step.

5. Watch your chosen scene again with the sound muted. Read all the parts of the dialogue to yourself as the video plays silently. Don't get ahead of or fall behind the pace of the film—try to lip-sync each actor's part.

You'll be impressed by this exercise for several reasons. Not only will you reap the benefit of the screenwriter's words, but also a director's influence on how those words are accompanied by pictures and action. Not to mention the effect of the language spoken by professional actors. All the decisions about word choice, diction, timing, emphasis, pace, and pauses—how everything comes together and flows in the performance. All without narrator intrusion. In plays especially, dialogue carries the story rather than special effects. Learn from them.

You could probably quote a dozen lines from current movies, lines that have become catchphrases that fall into use, then overuse in the popular culture. I think even more remarkable are those simple, plain language expressions that strike sparks in your recollection because the wording is distinctive, and you connect them instantly with images from a film, a play, or even a superb piece of fiction.

That's the kind of dialogue you should be striving to write. Memorable dialogue.

keeping track of CHARACTERS

Your fictional world must be peopled. And with distinctive, interesting, realistic characters, if you please. Even if those characters are Antz and Bugs. Before you get far in creating a world full of fictional denizens, you'll want a way to keep track of them. The better organized you are at the outset, the fewer of your creative resources you will have to spend just finding materials you mislaid. So use some form of ...

THE CONCORDANCE

This is your treasure chest of information on characters, settings, and background for your stories. Depending on the quantity of your research, this might either be in a file folder, a document box, or an entire filing cabinet. I recommend one tool above all other—simple index cards, five-by-eights like this one:

CHARACTER	☐ Master	☐ Major	☐ Minor	Role/Title:

Pertinent Bio	Physical	Distinctive Language
. . . .	Ht/Wt	. . . .
. . . .	Hair	. . . .
. . . .	Eyes	. . . .
. . . .	Nose	. . . .
. . . .	Mouth	. . . .
. . . .	Hands	
. . . .	**Striking Feature**	. . . .
. . . .		. . . .
. . . .		. . . .

Goal/Motivation	– Fatal flaw	. . . .
1.		. . . .
2.	+ Saving grace	. . . .
3.		. . . .
4.		
Name:		**Age:**

I tape the tops of them inside a file folder, overlapping, so only the name line at the bottom shows for all but the top card. The piece of tape acts like a hinge. When I want to add a detail or recall the color of a character's eyes, I just flip up the hinged cards above the one I want.

Filling in the blanks is a no-brainer. Except for human goals and motivations, which are discussed in detail on pages 92–95.

I don't recommend you write entire biographies of each person in your novel before you begin the story. That's because I'm lazy. I'd rather write story than genealogy. Also I tend to fall in love with my own research and might try to include an entire biography in my story — material that doesn't advance the plot.

A THOUSAND *words* ARE WORTH ...

THE FIRST 1,000 WORDS MILESTONE

The purpose of these words is to create a lasting first impression on an editor or agent. The word *compelling* gets a lot of mileage in lines pulled from critical reviews. But here I mean it quite literally.

Your first 1,000 words must compel an editor or agent past the milestone where she would normally reject a manuscript. The deeper you can force a publishing professional to read into your novel, the greater the likelihood she will eventually be invested deeply enough to buy or represent it.

Use this checklist to evaluate your work's first 1,000 words:

FUNCTIONS OF THE FIRST 1,000 WORDS

❏ Introduce the heroic character and give clear signals about his personality, appearance, flaws, and strengths. In other words, begin to characterize him, a process that will continue throughout the novel. Force your reader to care about this character.

- [ ] Introduce, or at least allude to, the heroic character's worthy adversary. Characterize her as well.

- [ ] Present or strongly suggest the surpassing conflicts of the story. You should have several, but certainly the most important should come into play early.

- [ ] Deliver evidence of the danger, suspense, or dramatic irony you might have hinted at in the first 100 words.

- [ ] Remain true to the tone and mechanics of the first 100 words.

- [ ] Foreshadow crucial scenes to come in the first 50 to 100 pages, the point-of-no-return complication.

- [ ] Foreshadow the climax in some way.

- [ ] Flesh out the setting.

- [ ] Demonstrate your ability to write at least one scene filled with action, conflict, imagery, and dialogue. If your first 1,000 words simply used narration and exposition—explained the background, described people or settings, and philosophized about action that will come in later chapters—you haven't a prayer of escaping the inevitable rejection. Done properly, that is, maintaining singularity, your scene could make an editor or agent believe your project could make money.

- [ ] Establish a clear central story line (what I call singularity) so the reader knows, or thinks she knows, where the story will go.

- [ ] No matter how serious your drama, elicit a couple of smiles and at least one laugh from your reader.

- [ ] Create *Oh, wow!* moments at intervals, at least once on every other manuscript page or so.

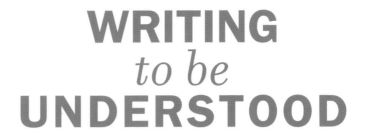

WRITING *to be* UNDERSTOOD

What constitutes an effective sentence?

In a word, comprehension. No matter how creative and poetic your writing, if nobody understands it, it might as well be a diseased elm falling in empty forest. So let's focus on comprehension as we talk about writing style. Comprehension begins with choosing comprehensible, precise words, which we've already discussed. How you put those words together is called effective writing.

The single most important lesson in writing effectively

One factor affects sentence comprehension more directly than any other. Simplicity. And nothing contributes to simplicity like brevity. The shorter a sentence, the greater the comprehension. Period.

When I taught basic reporting to military journalism students for the Department of Defense, I came across a comprehension scale that measured the ability of newspaper readers to understand sentences of varying length. I don't remember the source of the study and I haven't been able to dig it up in my research. But because it had such an effect on me, I remember it so clearly I can reproduce it here with no trouble.

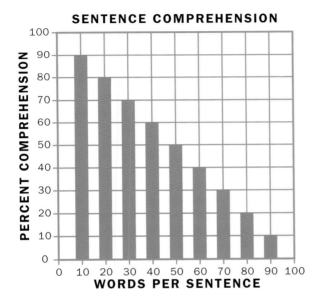

SENTENCE COMPREHENSION

(graph: PERCENT COMPREHENSION vs WORDS PER SENTENCE)

READING COMPREHENSION IN TERMS OF WORDS PER SENTENCE

At one extreme, the scale tells you that reader comprehension of one-word sentences was 99 to 100 percent. At the other extreme, readers comprehended 100-word sentences at the 1 percent level or less. I know what you're thinking … Isn't that self-evident?

Perhaps. But don't stop there. Hold the illustration at arm's length. Notice the nearly straight line formed by the ends of the bars indicating that the longer the sentence, the less the comprehension. You don't often find correlations as direct as this outside mathematics.

DOES THIS mean YOU SHOULD WRITE FICTION
FULL OF one- TO TWO-WORD sentences?

Hardly. I'm giving you a tool that you can forever implant in
the photographic memory section of your fiction-writing brain.
From now on, every time you write a sentence, call up that picture. If the sentence you write comes to 25 words, you can
assume—as a guide—that your readers will comprehend 75
percent of your communication. If you write 50-word
sentences—all other things being equal—expect readers to
comprehend only half of what you write. If you dare to write
75-word sentences, you know the percentage of comprehension
you can expect to achieve.

WHAT ABOUT THAT WRITING ADAGE THAT SAYS:
WRITE TO SUIT YOURSELF AND NOT SOME
FICTIONAL "reader"?

Forget that rule for the moment. We're talking about comprehension. You can't afford to alienate readers who can't decipher your message. I give you these basic comprehension tools
as a starting point for simplicity of style, which leads to greater
understanding of your words and ideas among the greatest
number of readers. Don't forget, the greater your readership,
the more books you will sell.

Popular novelists do write sentences of 40 words or more.
But rarely back-to-back. You most often find a long sentence
bracketed by short ones.

Variety. Diversity. Rhythm.

*Choose your own term,
but in general, write in short,
direct sentences
for the sake of the people
who might be more willing to buy
your books if they can
understand what you're writing.*

NARRATION
versus
SCENE-ERY

HOW can I know when to use narration instead of writing a scene?

To begin, narration is a handy way for the author to give information, create atmosphere, develop setting, and provide data that would take too long to portray in the action of a scene. Like scenes, narration must move the story forward, carrying an audience from one scene to another. The best narration is full of images, implied conflicts, and promises of tense moments to come in the story. But ...

Narration is often too handy, too easy to write. It can make a writer lazy because she can empty her thoughts and opinions on the page. She can rely on telling the story in a kind of movie voice-over without letting characters interact and play out the story. Scenes require work because you have to bring people to life and create realistic situations that speak for themselves.

RULE OF THUMB: Write Ten Master Scenes that carry the central story from beginning to end. Add more of these scenes if you must. Then use other types of scenes to carry subplots and to move readers between Master scenes. Finally, if gaps remain between any two scenes, you can build a bridge of narration to carry your audience.

As you try to decide between using a scene or using narration to make a point, here's something to consider:

THE WRITER'S SHORT TEST FOR DETERMINING WHEN TO USE NARRATION

❑ Use narration when it's the most economical way to move a story forward and a Master or Major scene isn't called for. (See pages 42–43 for more details about Master and Major scenes.)

❑ Never use narration in place of significant action that affects a significant character.

Have you ever read one of those stories in which the hero hears that the villain was killed offstage while the hero was in pursuit? You feel cheated by the author who didn't show the action but rather told it. Don't do that.

WRITING
creatively

They want a fresh experience. They want you to invent. You don't have to make up a new language, as in *A Clockwork Orange*. There's no need to go experimental, either, writing in accents or phonetics to the point where the writing feels alien.

Rather, readers want to see familiar words used in fresh ways. And they want to read good stories told in creative ways. You must entertain, provoke, and excite your readers with your creative genius. You get to the top of this writing game when you *Wow!* your readers with words and stories. You just cannot do that without a passion to invent.

Not to dwell on the dark side of this point, but you must at least avoid what I call the death knell of creativity: automatic writing. I'm talking about the stuff you read in most papers, the junk you grind out at work, the utter mind-numbing trash that you find on 96.04683 percent of Web sites in America.

*You'll never master
the art of giving readers
what they want if you settle
for the first words
that slither through your fingers
onto the keyboard.*

RULE OF THUMB: Avoid automatic writing. If it's coming too easily, beware. It might not be the muse in you talking, but the garbage man.

THE
writing
SAMPLE

IF an EDITOR LIKES MY FIRST 1,000 WORDS, DOES THAT MEAN SHE'S GOING TO BUY MY NOVEL?

Not likely, but you're on the right track. She'll likely read on and ask for a larger writing sample, say your first fifty pages, which is about 10,000 words.

Mission of the Writing Sample: To engage an editor or agent so strongly he will read the entire sample and ask for the complete manuscript. Reading an entire manuscript from an unknown is a significant investment of that publishing professional's second most valuable resource, time. That's why they often ask for the sample first. Make those 10,000 words count.

CHECKLIST FOR THE FIRST 10,000 WORDS (FIFTY PAGES)

❏ Maintain those qualities of writing and storytelling you established in the first 1,000 words.

❏ Force the reader to fall in love with your heroic character, creating the feeling that the reader will share personally in any of his joys, perils, and griefs.

❏ Create a cast of distinctive minor characters and unforgettable major characters.

- [ ] Maintain singularity, that continuous central story line, while texturizing with relevant subplots. By page fifty, you should have set up every piece of action that is to come, especially the climactic scene.

- [ ] Entrap your main character in the central conflict of the story so firmly that he has passed a point of no return. By the time your story has reached fifty pages, the titanic clash between the heroic character and his worthy adversary should be inevitable. That a struggle will occur is no longer a question— only its timing, the extent of its violence, and its outcome remain in doubt. For you, the writer, what's left is the suspense and art you employ in compelling your audience to the climactic moment of your story.

- [ ] Every now and then, relieve the dramatic tension with an occasional smile or laugh.

- [ ] Firmly establish the expectation of that sense of *Oh wow!* once every few pages.

The most critical element of the first 10,000 words has everything to do with your heroic character.

THree InDISPenSaBLe E's For THe FIrST FIFTY PaGeS

1. **Establish** your heroic character unequivocally as the focal point of the story, no matter how complicated your plot.

2. **Endear** your heroic character inseparably to your readership, even if she is cursed with a flawed personality.

3. **Entrap** that heroic character inextricably in the central conflict.

READING
ease

I once studied samples from novels of best-selling writers and found that the top pros average better in several statistics than do non-best-sellers, amateurs, corporate, and government writers. As a rule, the best-sellers use shorter sentences, shorter words, and a higher percentage of the active voice. When these factors are analyzed in two top-selling word programs, I arrived at what I call the Reading Ease Ideal.

THE READING EASE IDEAL — MS WORD

MICROSOFT WORD
(USING READABILITY CHECK)

Words per sentence (avg):	**15** maximum
Characters per word (avg):	**4.5** maximum
Passive voice:	**5%** maximum
Flesch Reading Ease:	**80%** minimum
Flesch-Kincaid Level:	**6** maximum

THE FIVE GOALS OF THE REI: MS WORD

- **Average number of words per sentence.** Shoot for an average of 15 words or fewer to increase reading ease. Readers digest short sentences best.

- **Average number of characters, that is, letters of the alphabet, per word.** Your writing should average 4.5. Short words boost reading ease like no other factor.

- **Passive voice.** Limit your use of the passive to 5 percent or less.

- **Flesch Reading Ease.** This is the first of two scales you can find in MS Word to test reading ease in your writing. This scale runs from 0 percent to 100 percent. The higher the percent, the better the reading ease. Strive for 80 percent or higher.

- **Flesch-Kincaid Grade Level.** This scale measures reading ease as a number from 1 to 12. As a rule, the lower the grade level in a piece of writing, the better the reading ease. In MS Word, use the ideal of 6. Or lower. Forget about the notion of grade levels—just treat the number as a goal.

Another word processing program, WordPerfect, measures word length, sentence length, and use of the passive voice just as Word does. It reports in different terms, but with the same effect. Look here.

THE READING EASE IDEAL — WP

WORDPERFECT
(USING GRAMMATIK)

Words per sentence (avg): **15** maximum

Syllables per word (avg): **1.5** maximum

Passive voice: **5%** maximum

Sentence complexity: **30** maximum

Vocabulary complexity: **15** maximum

THE FIVE GOALS OF THE REI: WP

☐ **Average number of words per sentence.** Same as Word. Shoot for an average of 15 words or fewer.

☐ **Average number of syllables per word.** Your writing should average 1.5 syllables or fewer to achieve the ideal reading ease.

☐ **Passive voice.** Same as in Word. Limit your use of the passive voice to 5 percent or less in all your writing.

☐ **Sentence complexity.** WP measures sentence complexity on a scale of 0 to 100. Never exceed 30, no matter what. When you can, aim lower.

☐ **Vocabulary complexity.** This measures word length and numbers of syllables. For ideal reading ease, strive for a score of 15 or less on this 0 to 100 scale.

Turns out that it's not the vocabulary you own that matters. It's the vocabulary you use. You can use big words in your fiction. You should use them when no smaller word fits the precise meaning you want to achieve.

No matter which word processor you use, your intuition is trying to tell you there's something wrong with these goals, right? Too easy? Too direct? Relax. Use the REI goals in all your writing, edit with it, live with it. You won't regret it. Remember this: Best-sellers share these five traits, resulting in a high readability rate. Of these the most important factor in editing for reading ease is a low count of characters per word.

Edit your work a scene at a time until each scene achieves or surpasses every one of the five goals. When you exceed the goals of the REI, you will be writing at a level that surpasses most work that the average writer submits to an agent or editor.

Later, as you grow more assured in your writing, use bigger words and longer sentences to achieve an effect. For now, you can use the REI to boost the pace of all your writing.

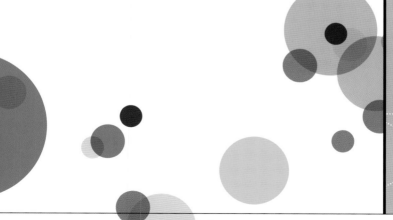

PACING *within* A SCENE

You've read writing how-to books that tell you to vary the length of sentences, the length of words, the length of paragraphs. This you can do by eye. You've also read that you should vary the pace of a story from scene to scene and within scenes. But nobody has told you how to measure pace.

Until now. Pick a scene, any scene, and we'll evaluate its pace and adjust it with this:

Use this tool to evaluate the pacing within a scene and to adjust pacing to suit your purpose. Here's how.

1. I'm assuming that you write your scenes as short stories within the novel. These short stories will have their natural beginnings, middles, and ends. Read your scene to find the natural break points between the beginning and the middle and between the middle and the end of the scene.

2. Again, make a copy of the scene and work on it in a separate file so you can preserve the original. Later you can copy and paste the edited version back into its place in the novel.

3. Mark your working text file at the breaks you identified. If you want to, on the right of the scale make notes to remind you where these breaks occur.

4. Next, analyze the text to get Reading Ease Ideal (REI) results (see page 66) for each of these three segments. Obtain a composite for each segment. MS Word users subtract the Flesch-Kincaid grade level from the Flesch score. WordPerfect users add the scores for sentence complexity and vocabulary complexity and subtract from 100.

5. Copy the results for your beginning onto the first scale of a copy of the Scene Pacing Tool (on page 70). The results for the middle go into the second scale. The results for the end segment of the scene go into the third scale.

6. Plug the result into the tool for your word processor for each segment—beginning, middle, and end.

7. Connect the dots to see how the pace flows through the scene.

8. Evaluate. Is the chart showing you what you want to see? Here are some guides to your evaluation.

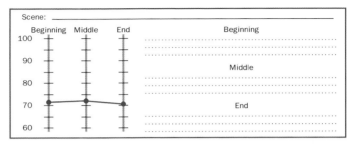

Level. The three segments of the scene don't vary much. Not a choice you'd want to make. Try editing to get some diversity into the scene until it looks like one of the following three choices.

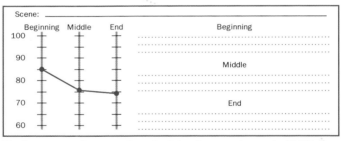

Peak pace at the opening. Is this what you intended? Higher intensity at the beginning, tailing off at the end? If so, check word count after the opening. You won't want a high-energy start that drones away into a never-ending scene.

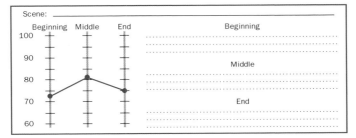

Peak pace at the middle. Action set up at the beginning, picking up the pace to a climactic, high-energy middle, with pace dropping off toward the end of the scene.

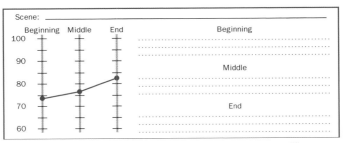

Peak pace at the end. This is a strong pacing choice. Here you can end a scene with your highest energy and use either a punch line or a cliffhanger to hold your reader as she goes into the next scene.

This is not to say that all your scenes should peak at the end. That doesn't help you in the variety department. You'll have to make the call on how to pace any given scene because only you will know how one scene fits with another. This tool will help you make informed decisions about each scene.

HOW TO *put a face* ON YOUR *characters*

Take a picture. Literally.

I take photographs for all my characters — clippings from magazines and catalogs. You can keep them in a file — I use plastic sleeves. Whenever you're writing a scene, lay out all the characters who play a part in the action. Look at them now and while you're writing to remind yourself when you want to use a detail about their appearance to enrich an image of them. By the way, you don't have to use photographs. Caricatures and other line drawings, even cartoons, work very well. Here's a twist:

Use faces from comic books. It isn't plagiarizing to borrow the face of, say, Peter Parker and put it into words to describe your novel's villain. In the comics, you get to see a whole range of emotions as the artists intensify facial features to dramatize.

Use stick-on notes to add name labels. Use larger notes to record extra details that you might not put on the character card (showed on page 53).

Cut out the photos and tape them to your character cards. You have your notes and pictures at hand anytime you want to create a physical image. This trick saves miles of writing notes.

You can brainstorm ways to dress your characters, too. This trick saves you from wasting valuable brain power on "thinking up" a character's wardrobe. Use fashion sources such as Abercrombie & Fitch, Victoria's Secret, *The New York Times* magazine and newspaper, Eddie Bauer, Sears, Kmart, and others for isolating the distinctive aspects of your character's dress. These specialty catalogs and sources tend to target different demographic groups. Since these retailers and direct-mail researchers have already done their homework, you can capitalize. Also, if your character has a sporting or hobby interest that involves specialized clothing or equipment, check out those catalogs.

Finally, find distinctive interests for your characters. Use the library, magazine racks, and the Internet to identify interesting, individualistic aspects of a character. Hobbies, tastes in clothing, furniture, food, drink, movies, books, and so on. Don't dump too much information at once. Create continuing threads and tie-backs that contribute to a feeling of a subplot. Don't be arbitrary about it; never drop details into the story for their own sake. Instead, bring those interests into play as part of the central story line, or at least a major subplot. Be authoritative. You can hardly paint your character as an expert on Central American aborigines if neither you nor she can name a single tribe. Do your homework or avoid the issue altogether.

CHARACTER

SIMPLICITY

WHAT'S THE BEST WAY TO KEEP A NOVEL ON TRACK?

Simplicity. Start simple, stay simple, avoid over-writing. I've known people to get to 200,000 words and not be anywhere near the ending. Unless you're Stephen King, that's a huge problem.

Simplicity endures. Don't worry about themes, metaphors, symbols, history, or complexity. Don't try to write great literature, message fiction, or meaningful prose. Tell a good story. The rest will take care of itself.

THE ELEMENTS OF SIMPLICITY

Borrowing heavily from *The Elements of Style* by Strunk and White:

❏ Write short sentences.

❏ Use the active voice.

❏ Let specific verbs and concrete nouns carry most of the freight.

❏ Get to the point in your sentences, paragraphs, and scenes.

❏ Respect the concept of singularity—a single idea to a sentence, a single topic to a paragraph, a single purpose to each scene, a single, dominant central story line to your work of fiction.

❏ Plan to simplify (even before you start writing). That is, you can't leave simplicity to the mercy of a good intention. Or to a cute saying like the KISS formula: Keep it simple, stupid. Write a work plan before you write your story. Set down your writing goals and objectives for the project.

In the beginning, lay out a straight path for your novel's central structure from beginning to end. The straightest, simplest possible path in story structure? The shortest distance between two points, A to X.

A ⟶ X

Where A is your opening scene, and X is your climactic moment near the ending. That's the skeleton of story, folks, the Opener and the Closer.

It's common to talk about story structures in terms of beginnings, middles, ends, complications, reversals, subplots, rising action, and all the rest. I've gone into some detail myself in discussions of writing. But, when you distill structure to only two elements, you always come back to the Opener and the Closer. If you write those two scenes first, at least in sketch form, you'll avoid a world of over-writing.

FORESHADOWING

You see this technique most often in film because Hollywood tends to be so obvious about things, often treating moviegoers as morons. In the movie *Braveheart*, an early scene of betrayal sets up the possibility of a pivotal betrayal at the climax of the story. And just to be sure that we didn't fail to get it, Mel Gibson's heroic character turns fatally stupid, allowing himself to begin to be duped so often in trusting men who can't be trusted that by the film's end, he deserves to die of terminal stupidity.

The trouble with this device is its familiarity, its tendency to give away the outcome of a critical scene. Once you sense that the climactic scene has developed the feel of an earlier scene, you know how the story is going to turn out. At least in flashbacks you see new information revealed, facts from the past that explain the present. When you see a scene being played out as you have already seen it, all you're getting is repetition. And a repetition that spoils the ending besides.

Once again, all writers use this technique, and I wouldn't dream of eliminating it from your own tool kit. Instead I have these ...

FORESHADOWING TIPS

1. If you must foreshadow by writing a big scene, do it no more than once. Don't assume that readers are too stupid to get the point. Too much foreshadowing of the same issue diminishes the effect of later scenes.

2. Foreshadow a major event that will involve the heroine by writing a similar, seemingly minor event into the life of a minor character. The players in your novel might not give the event more than a shrug until the larger, similar event plays out in the life of the heroine. The moment it happens everybody in the story—and your readers—will make the connection at once.

3. Introduce a surprise effect. You can add a delicious taste to your art by creating seemingly predictable situations, then springing unexpected results on your characters and readers.

I find the most stunning example of such a surprise in Larry McMurtry's *Lonesome Dove*. McMurtry develops his characters thoroughly and distinctively. But unlike most authors, he allows some of the best characters, both minor and major, to die horrible deaths. Yes, the bad guys often do get their just desserts. But all too often, to my tastes, the good guys also get their unjust desserts. It's all part of McMurtry's portrayal of the West as an unforgiving environment. And it sets up the violent death of one of modern fiction's most endearing characters. By the time that heroic character gets mortally wounded, so many others—good and bad—have gone before him, you can guess how things will turn out. You can only hope that the foreshadowing is a trick. And, I think, the ability of that novel to cause me to invest such hopeful emotion in it is the reason I always list it as one of my favorites.

HOW TO
write a
BEST-SELLER

THE NO-FAIL TOOL FOR WRITING A BEST-SELLER!
GUARANTEED!

Isn't that what everybody wants? The lazy man's way to riches?
And, if you don't mind, riches without raising a sweat. No
effort. No risk. Complete with a money-back guarantee.

Here is just the gimmick for you. If you use this tool faithfully, it could take you down the path toward writing riches.

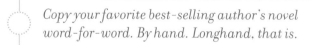

> *Copy your favorite best-selling author's novel*
> *word-for-word. By hand. Longhand, that is.*

Don't groan about being tricked. Give it a try.

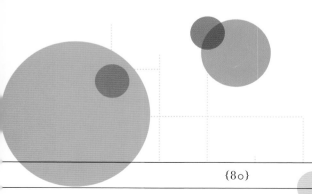

WHAT COPYING A BEST-SELLER CAN TEACH

☐ **Simple mechanics.** Things like punctuating dialogue.

☐ **Publishing conventions of the genre.** Chapter length. Narration. Story structure.

☐ **Writing action, conflict, imagery, and dialogue.** In the category of books you want to write.

☐ **How to economize on your novel's first draft.** Do this exercise long enough and you'll see how every word serves a purpose in a best-seller, carrying the freight without detours. In short, you learn how not to waste your own time and words.

CONSIDERATIONS WHEN COPYING A BEST-SELLER

☐ **Be wary of plagiarism.** You can't sell the words of another person. This exercise should help you master the techniques of the masters, not the exact words.

☐ **Don't transcribe mindlessly.** Pay attention to what the writer was doing and why.

☐ **Take notes as you copy.** Jot down the lessons you learn.

☐ **Don't copy an entire novel at once.** If you want to write breathless action like Dean Koontz in your climactic scene, select one of his novels and copy a suspenseful scene. Then write your own climax. Need your character to develop a distinctive identity? Pick up an Anne Tyler novel and follow one of her creations for a few scenes, copying every word Anne wrote about him.

You want to write?

Write.

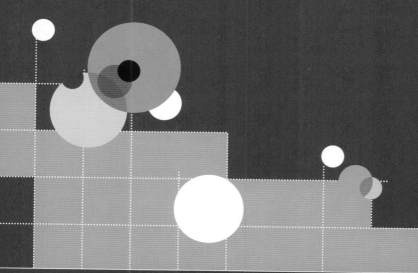

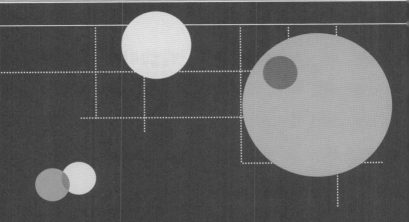

Don't wait for the muse.

Write.

Just plant your butt
in a chair and write.

NARRATION

WHO SHOULD TELL MY STORY?

Your narrator tells the story. It can be a character or a godlike character who chooses the words. The narrator can be neutral or involved.

THE neutral narrator

Should you work with a neutral narrator, try to be balanced. Don't use editorially charged words. Don't gush over good guys or condemn the bad guys. Don't sneak the author's opinions into the narrator's point of view. Move the story along by transporting readers from one scene to the next, where character actions and dialogue carry the freight.

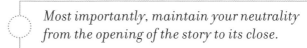

> *Most importantly, maintain your neutrality from the opening of the story to its close.*

Let the reader get her opinions from your characters. In this example, the narrator remains neutral, reporting only what happens:

> She shot him a look of disgust.
> "I'm sorry," he said. "I can't stop drinking. It's a disease. I'm sick. I'm—"
> She turned and stalked out of the room.

Compare this version, in which the narrator lets her neutrality slip:

> He was a disgusting mess, a hopeless drunk.
>   "I'm sorry," he said. "I can't stop drinking. It's a disease. I'm sick. I'm—"
>   Hopeless. She turned and stalked out of the room.

Does that mean the second version can't work? Not at all. You can read version two as if reading the mind of the woman in the scene. You might even argue that it's superior to the first point of view. I'm simply saying that the narrator in version one stands above the fray and reports what's going on in the scene. In version two, she participates in the scene. She's ...

THE JUDGMENTAL NARRATOR

The judgmental narrator offers endless possibilities for telling a story artfully just in the choice of her words. The narrator wears her opinion on her sleeve so readers can identify with her. Or even disagree.

> *And, in some of the most magical stories, the reader discovers that the narrator cannot entirely be trusted, adding a measure of uncertainty to the reading experience.*

Often the judgmental narrator tells the story from a first-person point of view of one of the characters, usually the heroic character. This gives a story an air of personal intimacy.

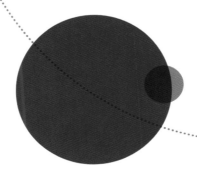

attitude

To me, the best stories are always stories with characters opposed to each other on attitude rather than circumstance alone.
For instance, the conflict between cop and criminal relies on
adversity between their career choices. But that conflict always
benefits tenfold when they have strong attitudes toward each
other as well.

> *No good story can exist*
> *without characters with attitude.*

By attitude, I don't mean bad attitude. I mean words, characters, and narrators who evoke a response, either attracting or
repelling us in some way. When such characters come off as
distinctive personalities, you're on the way to planting your
pennant on Mount Creativity.

Look at the three examples from my novel penned as John
Harriman, *Prelude to War*. The three different points of view
convey three different attitudes.

First, the narrator talking about the unsung hero:

> Nobody wanted to tiny talk with him anyhow. Because
> to talk to him you had to ... well, *look* at him. ... *Weird*
> *Science. Toad. Freak Show.*

Second, the POV of Captain Poole. The guy self-talks in street
language. Co-narrates his own scenes, man. Dig?

> *Night Runner, man.* Making the plays, making the peo-
> ple around him play better. *Da Larry Bird of Battle. Da*
> *Jason Kidd of Kombat. Da Wayne Gretzky of ... something-*
> *something.* Guy's mind always three moves ahead. See-
> ing the enemy in the empty spaces before they got there.
> Slipping up on the Ta-Ta-Taliban and—

Third, the POV of Saddam Hussein's food taster, whose voice and
attitude are far more conventional, though foreign-sounding.

> Karim-Assad saw that Saddam was looking him in the
> eyes. Never had he done such a thing before, not like
> this. In the past, if he did meet Karim-Assad's eyes he
> was only looking at Karim-Assad's belly through them.
> Did the taster's eyes betray any sign of pain, any onset
> of spasms? Only a belly. That's all he had ever been to
> Uncle Saddam, a distantly related belly.

THE
scene **CARD**

Your scenes are the building blocks of storytelling, of course.

The Scene Card can help you build your story in a number of ways.

First use a stack of cards to lay out the sequence of your story. Use the Ten-Scene Tool (seen on page 6) as a starting point to lay out the main events of the central story line. You should have ten stacks with subsequent scenes and perhaps subplots laid out beneath each of the turning points you identified on the Ten-Scene Tool.

For starters, just write headlines on each card. For instance, you might have an opener for your romance that goes:

> Josh meets Andrea at the funeral of her brother, whom
> he killed in a car wreck. She goes berserk.

Later you'll go back to write the scene using the checklist that follows. Once you have the headlines in place, you don't even have to write the scenes in order.

Just before writing the scene, use the checklist to sketch in the action. With that for a start, you'll find it easier to write.

Get busy.

SCENE CARD

❏ Master ❏ Major ❏ Minor

Characters in this scene:

_____ _____

_____ _____

_____ _____

Setting:

The scenes purpose is to:

❏ Move the master story line ahead
❏ Introduce or develop characters
❏ Introduce or worsen a problem
  (Defeat)
❏ Solve a problem (Victory)
❏ Set up later scenes
❏ Create atmosphere or
  develop setting
❏ Present information or data

What happens in this scene:

ACIIIDS INTENSITY SCALE—ELEMENT TO EMPHASIZE
(Circle one):

Then mark each scale with the intensity
of each element in the scene (at its peak):

ACTION	impending	overt	frenetic
CONFLICT	tension	open hostility	fatal
IMAGERY	suggested	telling	determinate
INVENTION	cheap trick	wondrous smile	WOW!
IRONY	subtle	visual	take your breath away
DIALOGUE	internal	debate	imbroglio
SUSPENSE	invisible	chapter show	nail-biter

PLAN OF ATTACK FOR WRITING SCENES

❏ Tell what happens in the scene. Identify the action, players, and setting.

❏ State the purpose of the scene. Which ought to help you ...

❏ Identify the type of scene you'll write: Master, Major, Minor (refer to pages 42–43).

❏ Identify a singular element to highlight: action, conflict, imagery, invention, irony, dialogue, or suspense.

❏ Write the scene in as few words as possible in the tiny space provided.

HOW TO TELL WHAT HAPPENS IN SUCH A SMALL SPACE

As you fill in the blank space, try to answer only the most pertinent of these questions in the space on the card:

❏ What will happen in this scene?

❏ Why will it happen?

❏ What earlier event caused this scene to happen?

❏ Whose motives drive the scene?

❏ Whose motives will those motives come into conflict with?

❏ Who are the characters who will play out this scene?

❏ What happens to each of them in the end?

❏ In what ways do they interact?

❏ Who is helped and harmed by the outcome?

❏ Who learned what lessons in this scene?

❏ Because of this outcome, what consequences will be felt later in the story?

❏ How does this scene point to the climactic moment of the story?

❏ What was the element of *Oh wow!* in this scene?

❏ What detail in this scene ties back to an earlier scene?

❏ What detail in this scene comes into play in a later scene?

That's a lot to answer in a very small space, but do the best you can. Use the back of the card. Just get down the headlines at first. Then develop the scene in detail in your manuscript, working from this card as your blueprint. Use the card to help you keep focus until you're done writing.

RULE OF THUMB: If you're trying to answer too many questions in a single scene, you probably need to focus on only the most important questions. Then use different, smaller scenes to answer the less important questions.

USE THE SCENE CARD TO STICK TO ONE STORY LINE AT A TIME

Here's an instance where you can learn from my experiences. Suppose you have a story that alternates settings and narrative points of view. The reader spends time with the hero, learning how she will achieve her worthy goal. Next the reader jumps to the lair of the villain to see how the hero's quest will be thwarted. This style of story construction can create a terrific state of suspense and reader connections because a reader knows more than the hero.

But writing the story can be a nightmare if you try to alternate from one narrative viewpoint to another as you go. It is for me. So, I've stopped alternating as I write. I simply organize my cards to follow a single central story line at the very beginning of my book. Then I write that story line to its end, or at least well on the way toward the end.

I find it helps me find and maintain the character's voice. Best of all, it becomes the touchstone to all later story lines. When I'm writing the villain's POV, I know where he must go if he wants to confound the hero. I can identify points where the two will clash. I can integrate subplots.

This tip works for better writing. Give it a try.

WHY DO
good CHARACTERS
DO *bad* THINGS?

HOW DO I GIVE MY CHARACTERS QUALITIES THAT MAKE THEM BELIEVABLY MOTIVATED?

Short Answer: You give them distinctive goals and motivations.

Move your people to action by a variety of internal and external forces instead of just one plot event. That makes them real to readers.

Refer to the Character Card on the next page. At the lower left of the card, there are four lines for the goals and motivations you should consider as you add depth to the people of your story. I explain the four major motivators here. Use these to help you fill in those lines.

"MISSION-DUTY"

Motivations and Goals. Our patriotism, honor, loyalty, devotion—the better angels of our nature—drive us in idealistic ways. They're the reasons we stay faithful to friends and lovers, political parties, and other associations. They cause us to vote, write letters to the editor, and volunteer to feed the homeless one day a month at the city shelter.

Don't worry that the bad actors in your fiction might not find motivations in this category. Remember, every coin in the realm of the good has its evil side. Terrorists take patriotism to an extreme. And nobody claims to be more patriotic than the leaders of a coup d'etat. Republicans and Democrats engaged in political struggles often seek the same lofty goals but differ on the means.

"career-selfish"

Motivations and Goals. No matter what our mission, we usually have career and selfish considerations deeply enmeshed in them. For instance, a soldier enlists for patriotic reasons. That doesn't mean he wants to rush into a minefield to give his life for his country. And, in the course of serving, getting a few promotions along the way are usually strong motivations, too.

On the flip side, somebody who uses despicable tactics, such as extortion, racism, or sexual harassment to climb the career ladder clearly uses unpleasant, if not unlawful, means to achieve his goal.

CHARACTER ❑ Master ❑ Major ❑ Minor		Role/Title:
Pertinent Bio	**Physical**	**Distinctive Language**
. . . .	Ht/Wt	. . . .
. . . .	Hair	. . . .
. . . .	Eyes	. . . .
. . . .	Nose	. . . .
. . . .	Mouth	. . . .
. . . .	Hands	. . . .
. . . .	**Striking Feature**	. . . .
. . . .		. . . .
. . . .		. . . .
Goal/Motivation	**− Fatal flaw**	. . . .
1.		. . . .
2.	**+ Saving grace**	. . . .
3.		. . . .
4.		
Name:		**Age:**

"Romance-sexual"

Motivations and Goals. To love and be loved, from the most platonic sense to the most devious. Somewhere along that spectrum, you ought to be able to place your characters. In a romance, a hero's goal might be marriage to the heroine. And the hero's worthy adversary might be trying every bit as hard, not to woo her, but to take her in a much more sinister sense.

"Quirks"

Motivations and Goals. I wouldn't want to overstate the case for kinky motivations. But face it, everyone you know is an eccentric in some sense, however large or small. Jeffrey Dahmer and Hannibal Lecter fit on one end of the spectrum. Your neighbor, who seems to have a funny gait but only because she refuses to step on cracks in the sidewalk, walks at the opposite end.

You needn't stretch everybody's quirk to the bizarre as you populate your story. Unless you want it to look like a barroom scene in one of the *Star Wars* movies. Look to real life for a sense of proportion. Although you can name a quirk in anybody, not everybody is ruled by quirks. Most of us keep our kinks under control and out of sight. Those who don't hide these extreme eccentricities come off as sociopaths.

Of course you won't limit yourself to four categories of motivation. You'll create realistic, distinctive characters with a full range of feelings and experiences. Breathe life into your characters with an attitude that these people existed before you began writing your story about them. Indeed, cultivate an attitude of someone lucky enough to be privy to a wonderful true story that you are obliged to tell within the framework of a play, a film, or a novel.

When you reveal character traits as if they have always existed—as opposed to making them happen because they need to happen in a timely way to make your story click—your story will work.

Think about it. Haven't you ever met somebody who seemed unpleasant on the surface, somebody who made the first impression that caused you to pinch your nose shut? Then, later, didn't you ever discover a brilliant, witty personality underneath that unpleasant exterior? And how many times have you met the all-American man or woman who, in a succession of situations, proved to be utterly treacherous? Of course you have. And that process of discovery should give you a clue to character creation.

> *Great fictional characters come to life when they are motivated by the same things that cause a given behavior in your own life.*

How a writer reveals a character—a bold slash here, a broad stroke there, a stipple, a dash, a mention, a flash, an image, a thought, a tic, a misstep, an act of bravery, a moment of cowardice, a wink, or a smile—contributes to the reader's sense of fictional reality.

WRITING
unique
STORIES

Some writers rebel at the notion of any kind of writing how-to book. They say that every writer has to be unique, that to be a success, a writer has to be different. So, by their logic, following advice in books is a one-way trip to formula and sameness.

I can see their point. I agree with it to some extent, too. But I don't get hung up on it. Readers expect conventions. Standard grammar and correct spellings, for two. But more than one best-seller has violated even those conventions.

> *Still, as a rule, a new novelist has to give readers—especially first readers, editors, and agents—what they expect. Good stories told so well and without gimmicks that they rise to the top of the piles of slush that inundate agencies and houses.*

Use this little checklist as a helper in keeping you from getting to the top without going over the top.

CATALOG OF ACCEPTABLE STRANGENESS

- [ ] Characters so odd but likable, you want to meet them
- [ ] Dangers so weird but so familiar, you're afraid they might happen in your own life
- [ ] Techno-possibilities so fascinating you're not sure whether they're fact or fiction
- [ ] Language so inventive, so graceful, so slightly off-key that it could only have written by a complex genius—yet simple and elegant enough so you understand it
- [ ] Ideas so powerful you wish you'd thought them first, yet you're grateful that the writer introduced them to you because they might make a difference in your life
- [ ] Tragedy so avoidable that nobody but a human being like you would allow it to occur
- [ ] Humor so fresh and original that all the popular sitcoms will steal it in the coming season
- [ ] Stories so personal that you grieve or rejoice as if they happened to you

CREATIVITY

ADVANCED *word* INVENTION EXERCISE

Here's a little drill I often give to writers in workshops:
Finish this sentence with the first word that comes to mind.

Thin as a _____.

Hurry up now; don't think about this too much.

So, what'd you get? Dime? Rail? Stick? Reed?

Very likely. That's what most of my workshop people get in the measly ten seconds I give them. Doesn't matter. When you're writing a first draft, any of those words will do. Any one of them that fills in the blank gives us what, class? Why a cliché, of course. I never get uptight about writing with clichés in drafts. In my book (to use one cliché), clichés are great shorthand devices when you're putting ideas on paper in a hurry. Because to me ...

> *Writing is way overrated. The truly creative writer gets the most mileage out of editing and revising.*

So let's get busy revising. Give me a list of at least a dozen alternatives to your first cliché. Just fill out Column A.

COLUMN A	COLUMN B	COLUMN C
Thin as (a) _____	_____	_____
Thin as (a) _____	_____	_____
Thin as (a) _____	_____	_____
Thin as (a) _____	_____	_____
Thin as (a) _____	_____	_____
Thin as (a) _____	_____	_____
Thin as (a) _____	_____	_____
Thin as (a) _____	_____	_____
Thin as (a) _____	_____	_____
Thin as (a) _____	_____	_____
Thin as (a) _____	_____	_____
Thin as (a) _____	_____	_____

Different deal, huh? Now you have to press, eh? But you still finished, right?

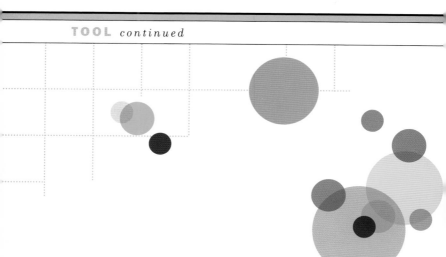

Now give me a dozen more in Column B.

Done? Now fill in Column C.

Done? You filled in thirty-six alternatives, right?

Or not. In which case, I'm thinking: Don't give up the day job before you go into writing creative fiction for a living.

Here's a tale for you to consider: In a workshop with corporate communicators, I asked them to give me sixteen terms for the phrase, *wrote quickly*, which came out of that specific-word exercise. In a room of about twenty people, not one was able to get a dozen after my best prodding. I went back to my hotel room that night thinking I'd asked too much of the class. I sat down and began writing quickly myself. In no time I had more than two dozen. Not because I was a genius, but because, unlike the corporate writer, I wasn't afraid to bend rules into pretzels. I *keyboarded at 120 wpm* and *dictated in speech-to-text software at 200 wpm* and *signed* (as in sign language with fingers flying) and *air-typed* and even *bibbled*, which sounds like nonsense even after I remind you that Mozart in *Amadeus* "scribbled and bibbled" in one of his lines.

Which is to say, corporate writers are used to wearing the straightjacket of rules and policies and VIP guidance. That works fine in the world of suits. For fiction, you have to loosen up. You have to shrug off that belted shirt to release your creativity. Which is to say …

> *Creativity demands that you risk ridicule as you push the envelope of your writing.*

Now I suppose I've insulted you. You've gone back and filled in all the blanks. Good. Congrats. You spewed the quantity of responses I asked for. Now let's look at quality.

For instance, you might have generated a whole family of clichés such as thin as a: dime, whip, or stick. Or you might have taken coin images to a new level, as in thin as a: penny, nickel, quarter, and so on through pesos, dinars, and drachmas. Fine. Just what I asked you to do.

But was it creative enough?

Not likely. Which is why I give you the Creative Writer's Bracketing Tool on page 134.

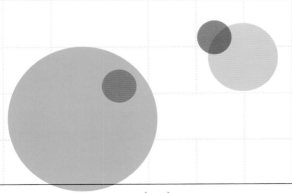

USE
short WORDS

You've heard that advice before. Now I'll give you some data to back it up. In ten novels that I studied, analyzing representative writing samples, I found word length is the factor that most often distinguishes successful novelists from amateur writing.

> *Best-selling novelists consistently use shorter words than non-best-sellers. It's a main reason their writing reads at a faster pace than most mid-list books.*

I analyzed these samples using MS Word's readability statistics, which will report on word length in average characters per word. During editing tests of my own writing I found that no other factor affects reading ease more than cutting long words down to size.

The samples from the best-sellers I studied averaged 4.21 characters a word. Other samples I analyzed for comparison averaged about a full character more. In the worst corporate writing samples I studied, it's common for samples to average more than 6 characters per word. In academic journals, writing is so dense as to be unreadable at more than 7 letters per word. As a naked number you might think that an average of 5.2 letters in a word is a trivial difference from the best-selling average of 4.21. It isn't.

RULE OF THUMB: Edit your writing to arrive at an average of 4.5 characters per word. If you use WordPerfect's Grammatik feature, edit until the average "syllables per word" score is 1.5 or lower.

Even the most elementary word count program will count words and letters or characters in your writing sample. From there it's a simple calculation to divide the total number of words into the total number of characters to arrive at an average of the characters per word. If that's what it takes, do it.

Use this tool if you use no others in your writing. When you edit your own writing, you'll see the difference.

Take a sample of a thousand words or so and run your own analysis and edit down to the maximum score.

The bonus of this tool is this: For the first time, you'll have a standard by which to measure your writing as you edit. You'll have a goal to shoot for. As you grow more aware of the importance of word length to your readers, you'll start writing first drafts with short words.

This tool is going to make you a better writer. Count on it, pun intended.

STRUCTURING
THE *climax*

Your Closer is the most important scene in the novel, bar none. Yes, the Opener is critical, but only second in importance to the climax.

The Opener must impress an agent enough to ask for more pages to help him decide whether to represent your book. The Opener must impress an editor enough to force her to ask for more pages to help her decide whether to buy your book. The Opener must impress a reader to give in to an impulse to take your book home from the bookstore.

But, it's the climax that closes the deal for all three parties—that's partly why I call it the Closer. The editor who bought my first book said that after he decided he liked the opening fifty pages, he skipped right to the ending to see if I could deliver in the climax. Only then did he make an offer on the book.

To make your book a best-seller, it matters more to readers— lots and lots of readers—what they say after they put your book down than when they pick it up.

A CHECKLIST FOR THE CLIMACTIC CLOSER SCENE

Ask yourself these questions about your Closer:

☐ **Is this scene a titanic final struggle?** Blow away your readers. Simple as that. No scene that precedes the climax should be more exciting. This is the payoff.

☐ **Does the heroic character confront the worthy adversary?** Absolutely mandatory. No exceptions.

☐ **Is the conflict resolved in the heroic character's favor?** Not mandatory, but usually the most popular choice.

☐ **Does the heroic character learn an important lesson?** The most dramatic events of our lives teach our characters—and us—something of lasting value. Our scars cost us something, perhaps innocence or purity, but we also wear them as badges of learning. A reader who walks away from the novel with a so-what attitude will kill you in the word-of-mouth department.

☐ **Does the scene avoid coincidence or divine intervention?** Your heroic character's decisions and actions must decide the story's most crucial battle.

☐ **Does the scene introduce new material?** It shouldn't. Everything that appears in the climax should have been set up earlier in the story.

☐ **Does the scene rely on flashbacks?** Avoid them in the climax. Keep the story moving by action and dialogue.

☐ **Does the climax use exposition?** Explanation causes this vital scene to drag.

☐ **Is the conclusion logical?** Just as all that goes before should point to the climax, even if many signposts have been artfully concealed, all that flows from the climax should be reasonable. An ending with a twist is fine. But no tricks.

☐ **Does the climax leave us feeling a sense of wonder?** Contrary to the conventional wisdom about impressions, your novel will be judged by its final impressions not its first. What will readers tell their friends after they put down your story?

BOTTOM LINE

☐ You must create a climactic Closer scene that surpasses any other scene in the novel in terms of action, conflict, imagery, and dialogue.

☐ Blow your readers away with the height and depths of emotions you achieve.

☐ Tattoo the outcome of your story on their brains and hearts forever.

☐ Leave them feeling disadvantaged that they might never meet your heroic character unless you write another novel featuring her.

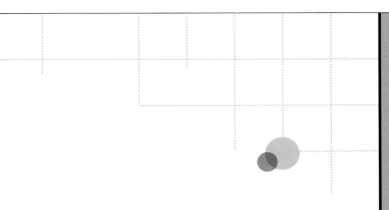

STRUCTURING TIP

Review your Ten-Scene Tool (on page 6) before you write the climax and after you finish, as a way of evaluating your story. Go back and look at the central events of the main story line and make sure they lead to your logical climax of events. If necessary add new intermediate scenes to clarify the story line. Or revise existing scenes to make the connections ring true.

BOTTOM-BOTTOM LINE

The editor who bought my first novel liked the Opener, the first fifty pages, the scenes that dragged him into the story.

But he made his buying decision on the climax, the closing pages, the Closer.

All that middle stuff. All the subplots. All the magic I thought I was using to keep up the interest through the story—he skipped it. Went right to the end.

Is it any wonder that I emphasize beginnings and endings? I'm conditioned by that experience forever. I hope that you will not have to relearn the lesson in your own writing life. Rather, that you will learn from my experience. Endings first.

CATEGORY
fiction

SHOULD I TRY TO BREAK INTO PUBLISHING BY
WRITING GENRE FICTION, THE SMALLER CATEGORY
BOOKS LIKE SCI-FI, MYSTERY, ROMANCE, OR HORROR?

It's an ongoing debate that'll never be settled. Dean Koontz says he regrets writing genre fiction because he was pigeon-holed for a long time and not accepted as a "big-book" author. Yet his bigger books were simply horror stories that transcended the genre.

Still: If you're looking to break in, it's often easier to do so in one of the genres. Editors will throw five thousand to ten thousand dollars apiece at ten romances, if they show promise of a strong, popular series. But they won't spend five hundred dollars on any mainstream novel that doesn't figure to be a sure thing at making the big-time. No editor wants her books ending up on the mid-list.

So you might consider launching your career as a package, aiming for category fiction. Think of a package as a distinctive idea kit that an editor can use in reselling to an identifiable reading audience.

THE CONTENTS OF A PACKAGE

❏ A concept recognizable to readers of category fiction, say, a Western.

❏ A concept that lends itself to functional artwork. The covers of Westerns speak of buckskin shirts, horses, cattle, sweeping landscapes.

❏ A concept that publishers can serialize. A series of stories about smaller quests within one huge quest to conquer the land, the outlaws, the robber ranch barons.

❏ A concept that permits a continuing cast of characters and settings.

❏ Perhaps most important, a concept that is fresh. A twist that nobody has exploited before, perhaps a magician turned cowpoke. It could happen. Might be a heck of a set of stories.

DO YOUR RESEARCH ON GENRE FICTION

❏ Identify the top three superstars within the category. How many books appear with their names on them each year? Do their books make the best-seller lists for category fiction regularly?

❏ Find out how the best-sellers are alike. Can you spot the similarities in those books using the checklist for a package?

❏ Discover what stands out as unique. How does each package differ from author to author and book to book? Can you identify other distinctive features of top writers?

❏ Resolve not to emulate any of these top sellers, either in their writing or their story lines. If you give the appearance of creating a knockoff, you're buying an express ticket to rejection.

❑ Develop a package that is fresh, distinctive, inviting, and capable of making an editor's career (and, not incidentally, your own), yet one that is also recognizable as a package that will sell to the readership of the leading authors.

HOW TO DIFFERENTIATE AN IDEA

❑ Take the idea into either history or the future. The *Star Wars* films have been called Westerns set in space.

❑ Combine two categories. Western-romance is not a huge stretch, for instance.

❑ Incorporate technology, using the technology of magic or science or philosophy. Philosophy? Sure, remember the *Kung Fu* series?

❑ Reflect the headlines. You could spin off a Western from the post Corps of Discovery explorers now popular in the bicentennial commemorations.

❑ Reflect trends in popular culture. Gang warfare, serial crimes, fashion trends, diet fads, anti-smoking militancy—all these modern phenomena would be fun to exploit in a period Western setting.

CAUTION: Those last two bits of advice invite you to tread thin ice. Headlines and trends fade fast. Publishers routinely take a year to get a book out after you deliver a first-draft manuscript.

Reasons to Write Category Fiction

Finally, as a writer of category fiction, I can tell you one very good reason to get involved with it. It's a terrific training ground.

First, it demands that you write more than one book, which develops a healthy attitude toward deadlines, word length, and story construction.

Second, it allows you to develop continuing characters from one title to the next in the series. As you mature as a writer, your characters will develop as well. You'll fill in bits of background. You'll round out aspirations. You'll fall in love with certain people, whether heroes or villains, as you see your readers develop interest in them.

Third, you get the luxury of working on a small stage, learning how to handle issues of scale. If you deal well with the smaller themes and narrow scopes, your editor and readers will ask you to write the big book.

When they do, you'll be ready.

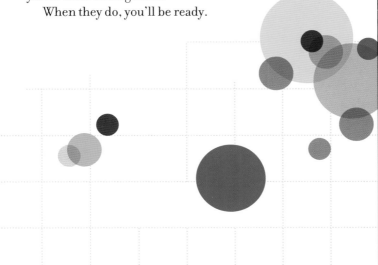

AVOIDING
bad
DIALOGUE

WHAT DOES BAD DIALOGUE SOUND LIKE?

Here are some general rules of thumb to avoiding bad dialogue.

Characters shouldn't "speechify." Be wary when a character talks past three lines. Break up long speeches with action, images, or conflict-laden responses from another character.

Don't let characters talk as we do in real life. Avoid chit-chat, such as:

> "How are you?"
> "I'm fine, how are you?"
> "Fine, I guess."
> "You guess?"
> "Yeah."
> "You gonna get to the point?"

That's what I want to know.

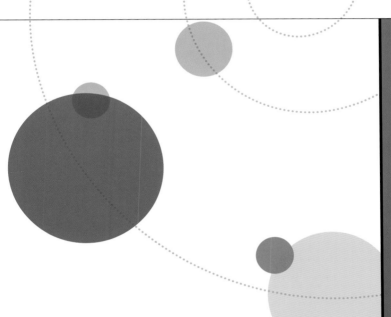

Avoid clutter. Let the dialogue flow. Read the following example:

> "Spit it out," she said, fiddling with his necktie.
>
> She seemed unable to make eye contact with him.
> That confirmed it for him. He thought he'd be on safe
> ground telling her why he'd been so cool toward her
> lately.
>
> He yanked the tie from her hands. "I don't trust you."
>
> He adjusted the knot and made sure the point of the
> tie touched the middle of his belt buckle.

Now look how well the same material reads when you cut the clutter:

> "Spit it out," she said, fiddling with his necktie.
> He yanked the tie from her hands. "I don't trust you."

EVERY SCENE *must* HAVE A PURPOSE

Use a scene card to identify the purpose of your scene.

SCENE CARD	What happens in this scene:
❏ Master ❏ Major ❏ Minor	
Characters in this scene: _____ _____ _____ _____ _____ _____	
Setting:	**ACIIIDS INTENSITY SCALE—ELEMENT TO EMPHASIZE** (Circle one):

The scene's purpose is to: ❏ Move the master story line ahead ❏ Introduce or develop characters ❏ Introduce or worsen a problem (Defeat) ❏ Solve a problem (Victory) ❏ Set up later scenes ❏ Create atmosphere or develop setting ❏ Present information or data	Then mark each scale with the intensity of each element in the scene (at its peak):

ACTION	impending	overt	frenetic
CONFLICT	tension	open hostility	fatal
IMAGERY	suggested	telling	determinate
INVENTION	cheap trick	wondrous smile	WOW!
IRONY	subtle	visual	take your breath away
DIALOGUE	internal	debate	imbroglio
SUSPENSE	invisible	chapter show	nail-biter

A scene might fulfill one or more purposes, although one must dominate all other purposes.

First of all, every scene must move the central story line ahead. Ultimately every scene points toward the climax. All scenes must fulfill this purpose to some extent. Here are some other purposes by category (see pages 42–43 for definitions of Master, Major, and Minor scenes):

PRIMARY PURPOSES OF MASTER SCENES

☐ Introduce or develop master characters acting and reacting.

☐ Portray a significant victory for a master character.

☐ Portray a significant setback for a master character.

PURPOSES OF MAJOR SCENES.

☐ Introduce or develop secondary characters; or develop master characters in lesser ways.

☐ Introduce or worsen a plot problem.

☐ Solve a secondary problem.

☐ Set up later Master scenes.

☐ Create atmosphere.

☐ Develop setting.

☐ Major scenes might also perform purposes listed below.

PURPOSES OF MINOR SCENES

☐ Develop major characters in small ways or develop minor characters.

☐ Create atmosphere.

☐ Develop setting.

☐ Portray information or data through action.

EFFECTIVE
sentences

Answer: Singularity. A sentence works best when it expresses a single idea, using no more words than necessary to express that idea.

Sentences come in a variety of shapes and forms. In high school you learned the terms simple, complex, and compound in defining sentence constructions. I'll redefine these terms because you're more interested in writer functions than sterile definitions.

Simple sentences

The effective simple sentence states a fact, portrays an act, or paints an image. The writer adds only minimal but relevant clarification. As always, the first job of such a sentence is to move a story forward, if not by action or conflict, then by an image that expands understanding.

> A sponge carpet of pine needles covered the trail. (an image of nine words)
>
> Bill grasped her arm. (action of only four words)
>
> A new fear chilled her skin. (six words of conflict)

Simple sentences send direct messages. And directness helps you maintain singularity. What's more, the message usually involves only one subject of the fact, act, or image—and often only one verb. These single-function constructions prevent lengthy explanations and awkward detours. Finally, simple sentences usually contain fewer words to get in the way of that single idea you want to sell in each sentence.

RULE OF THUMB: Write simple sentences of fewer than twenty words— an average of a dozen words is best. Write longer sentences if you must, but keep this rule of thumb in mind—and remember, the longer the sentence, the less the comprehension.

THE EMBELLISHED SENTENCE

I use this term instead of complex because, for our purposes, complexity is a negative. You begin with a simple sentence, adding one or more verbal clauses to expand or clarify the fact, act, or image of the single idea you want to communicate. Grammarians call these clauses dependent because they depend on the simple part of the sentence (independent clause) for meaning and cannot stand alone. I call them verbal clauses because, to my mind, the simple sentence part of the construction depends on them for additional meaning. A few grizzly examples will demonstrate:

> The carpet of needles cushioned the trail and absorbed the sounds of their footsteps. (fourteen words)
>
> She pointed at a looming hulk, which might have been just another shadow in the ink of night. (eighteen words)

Notice that the first part of each sentence (the first line in each pair) stands alone. The second part depends on something in the first part for meaning. No matter what form of sentence you write, keep in mind these ...

TWO PRINCIPLES FOR USING EMBELLISHED SENTENCES

1. No matter how complicated your embellished sentence, remember the concept of singularity. Keep to a single idea. If you wish to add a second idea to the one in that sentence, write a separate sentence.

2. Watch your word count. You often lose control of embellished sentences, especially in early drafts, adding redundancies, nuances, and explanations that weaken your writing.

RULE OF THUMB: Be wary of embellished sentences that exceed twenty words.

DOUBLED SENTENCES

Your English teacher called these compound sentences, ideas that could just as easily be two or more separate simple sentences.

Here's a doubled sentence with two distinct ideas, connected by *and*. Both ideas point to a singular problem. Each could stand alone:

> A rough pine bough slapped her face, and needles stabbed at her eyes. (thirteen words)

And here's a doubled sentence, connected by *but*, amplifying a single idea:

> She thought she might scream but nothing came out. (nine words)

RULE OF THUMB: Be wary of word counts that exceed twenty-five words in doubled sentences.

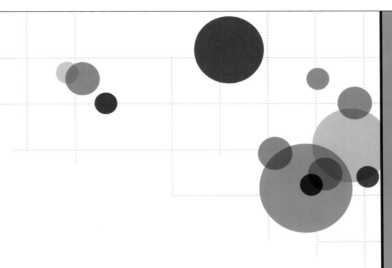

THE CONVOLUTED SENTENCE

Any sentence that violates singularity by treating two separate ideas, adding excessive nuance or explanation, or rambling. For example:

> Lord Smith-Piper had mandated that peasants could not hunt stags on the estate, which nestled like a caress between the meandering rivers, but Avery and his band didn't like rules and never abided by them. (thirty-five words)

You might think that a high word count alone would indicate the convoluted sentence. Not all. It isn't the words. It's the number of ideas, nuances, and explanations that will confuse a reader. Here we have one lord mandating, two rivers meandering, and three peasants not abiding.

Remember singularity and keep to a single idea, even in your most convoluted sentences.

THE *dark side* OF CHARACTER

HOW CAN I MAKE A CHARACTER
TRULY COMPELLING?

Reveal her deepest, darkest secrets, one tidbit at a time.

> *Each of us has something in his past. It makes
> us cringe to think about it. Something that
> we can't talk about with our lovers and clos-
> est friends.*

You can tap into the uneasy feelings caused by your own dark side. It isn't necessary to make fictional tale a personal confession to be effective. All you have to do is create a similar queasiness in your characters, especially if you can reach out from behind your work of fiction and generate the identical feelings in your audience.

Two examples come to mind from the same story, Thomas Harris's *The Silence of the Lambs*. One of Hannibal Lecter's intriguing qualities was the capability to identify that humiliating soft spot within other characters he interacted with. He rattled Clarice Starling, the FBI candidate played by Jodie Foster in the film, with his deductions about her upbringing, which she betrayed by the shoes she wore. The more we learned about Starling's secrets and fears, the more we admired her for overcoming that past. Ironically, we learn all of Lecter's most revolting past up front ("I ate his liver with some fava beans and a nice Chianti."). Yet, the secret that struck him at his heart was a sense of compassion he revealed near the climax of the story. For a moment, you might even have been willing to forget his repulsive past. Until he resorted to his vicious, cannibal tendencies, which jolted us back to the fictional reality of his persona.

You can evaluate each of your characters to find an extreme behavior, personality, or tendency that would lead to a character's dark secret. It might not even be necessary for that character to reveal such a secret—revelations along the way might give your readers enough evidence to form conclusions of their own.

Here I'll generalize:

Don't let anybody off the hook.

Your most heroic characters
as well as the most villainous have secrets.
That alone doesn't make them bad people,
only believable people.
And isn't that what you wish
to accomplish, after all?

Writing is way over-rated.

Revise and edit
until you're sweating
bullets, until your tenth draft
finally begins to read like an effortless
first draft.

Then cut it in half.

CHARACTER PoV

WHAT'S THE BEST TECHNIQUE I CAN USE TO WRITE LIKE THE PROS?

Let the reader see things through the eyes of the characters instead of the eyes of the author or narrator. Observe.

> He was tall, six-feet-two, with a nose to match, tall, thin, and straight.

That's the author talking.

> He caught sight of his six-feet-two reflection in the window of a bagel shop, paused, and studied his thin, straight nose both in profile and straight on. Straight on, he decided, always show his nose to her straight on. Never from the side.

Same information, different approach. One that gives the facts without stopping the story as if to say: *I'm going to describe somebody now.* At the small cost of a word increase, we see the reflection through the character's eyes, not the author's keyboard. We see action, both actual and implied—turning his head from side to side to study the profile is suggested. Plus we learn something about the character's personality. He's vain about his nose.

Here's another example of seeing through a character's eyes. In this brief scene only the characters do the talking.

> "You got a stiff neck or something?" she asked.
>
> "What?"
>
> "You keep turning your body instead of your head when you look at me."
>
> "What?"
>
> "Daddy?"
>
> "Honey, who is this guy?"
>
> "Not in the nose, Daddy, don't hit him in the nose."

The characters describe the action to one another, almost entirely between quote marks. The author—and narrator—stay out of the picture and let the characters react to each other and to events. You do your best writing when the people in the story make things happen. Naturally, there's nothing wrong with narration. What I'm saying with this example is that nobody, neither an author nor a narrator, interprets for the reader. Instead the reader interprets on her own.

One final example of seeing through a character's eyes:

> … the guy staring up at the center of my face makes me wonder if my fine, straight nose is going to leave the party in the condition it crashed the party. He's a full foot shorter than me, five feet and change, thighs like fireplugs, a chest like a beer keg, a pony keg stacked on top for a head—no neck.

Here the first-person narrator is described by creating the image of somebody else and showing the contrast. You learn that the narrator is six feet tall, plus change. He wonders whether his fine, straight nose will be broken. This technique shows us the image of it without actually letting on that we're describing it, a technique even better than the reflection thing, which tends to be a visual cliché.

texturizing
YOUR NOVEL

Here you employ the finest craft that you can to your writing to enrich your novel. You make connections, both subtle and obvious, between separate events in your novel, engaging the reader in the kind of interactive participation in the story that makes people rave about your fiction to other potential readers.

TECHNIQUES TO ENRICH YOUR NOVEL

❏ **Texturize using a seemingly trivial detail.** Writers often drop a small object or event into the narrative, especially early in the story. Left in plain sight, characters and readers overlook it until it comes into play at some critical moment late in the story. This technique works wonderfully when the detail isnt too obvious. In vintage films, the director would subject a detail like a burning cigarette in an ashtray to an extreme close-up. And in case we didn't get the possibility that it would later come to play an important part in the story, the soundtrack would hit a crescendo of ominous music to let you know somebody's in the room waiting to spring at the hero. Nowadays, you need to hire a crew of investigators to watch the film with you to pick up such minor details.

But the best trivial details work when they have been planted well enough so that when they crop up, you recognize them instantly and even give yourself a slap on the forehead for overlooking them earlier.

Usually, in writing a first draft, you don't have a handle on all the details, trivial or otherwise. That's what makes it so convenient to texturize with tie-backs. How do you do it? Simply go straight to the climactic or other important scenes of your story, usually toward the end of the book. Find a detail that's critical. Then look back in the book to see if you can locate an earlier spot to plant that detail in plain sight.

❏ **Texturize with seemingly small words and ideas.** I like this technique best of all the texturizing devices, because you can enrich the manuscript by using them in a number of variations. Here are two:

> **1.** Repeat a distinctive thought or phrase of dialogue in the story. This connects an earlier part of the story to a later one without having to rely on an overt transitional device. Television shows frequently overuse this technique, giving one character a pet phrase that he repeats ad nauseam. One way to vary the device is to give it a different meaning each time it's used. On *Seinfeld*, all the principal characters would use the same phrase, often with different meaning, all in the same scene, creating a device all its own.

> **2.** Plant the story's ending in the first thousand words. Simply review your ending. Transplant a telling word or thought directly into the beginning of the story. Massage the context so it doesn't become a crude giveaway, but rather a well-crafted throwaway line that turns out to be not so throwaway after all. Between the beginning and the end, don't fall victim to the temptation to continue hammering away on that singular thought or phrase. Let it lie. Clever readers will pick up on it.

☐ **Texturize using consistency of character.** Both motivation and cause and effect come into play during texturizing. Review each character's goals and motivations. Then take a look at every situation where the character comes into play. Satisfy yourself and your readers and make sure the character's behavior is consistent with her motivation. And that her consistently motivated behavior causes predictable effects. Look at small situations and the big events. Look for opportunities to reaffirm character consistency in the smallest ways.

Finally, look for changes as characters develop, either growing or deteriorating. Characters often do change. Your job as writer demands that any change is consistent with sufficient motivation and not just a whim of the author. Then, once that change is established, decide whether the character remains consistent to the end of the story. Or whether she backslides. Both are elements of effective texturizing.

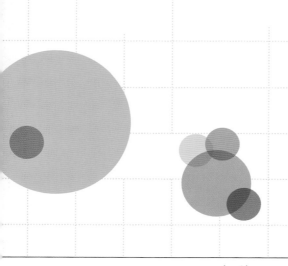

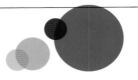

☐ **Texturize using conflicting points of view.** When you tie back characters who are in conflict to an event that involved both of them, look for opportunities to show how they differ in their recollections. When a significant event occurs within a novel, it should not be forgotten by the characters. And characters in conflict should remain in conflict even during the memory of that earlier scene.

☐ **Texturize using that element of surprise.** As you revise your fiction, take a close look at scenes that might be too methodical, too predictable. It's one thing for you to remain true to plausible motivation and believable cause and effect. It's quite another for your story to plod forward, technically correct but boring.

I'm not talking about trick endings where you unmask the narrator as the heroic character's pet kitten. That's too stupid for words. And I don't mean you should pull the rug out from under your readers at the climactic scene or major moments.

Rather, I suggest you find an unexpected ending to a scene, an unpredictable sentence to finish off a paragraph, or an unusual word choice to color a sentence. Surprise your readers. Better yet, surprise your characters. Best of all, when you can, surprise even yourself.

If you use this checklist faithfully as a way of looking at your writing, you will find ways to improve it, moving down the path toward your "big book." Even if you don't sell the piece in a "big book," in the end you'll have improved the quality of your work.

EDITING
using the
READING
EASE IDEAL

The REI tool (on page 66) gives you numerical goals to shoot for when you edit your work. Five simple objectives to guide you in revision. Just select a scene and let your word program run its magic. In any area where your work falls short of the ideal, edit and re-edit until it meets all five objectives. Before long, you'll see an improvement in the quality of your first draft scenes. The Reading Ease Ideal Tool forces you to:

☐ **Focus on a clear, measurable standard.** You can measure your editing progress with it. When your readability falls to 50 percent in a high-action scene, you sense that it drags. When you pep it up to 79 percent, you give it legs. When you pump it into the 90s, you know it sings. You don't have to rely on some vague scale like, *It sounds good to me.*

☐ **Cut out your darlings.** If you can't hit your ideal readability marks without deleting a lovely purple phrase, you will, as Paul Verlaine said, "Take eloquence and wring its neck" in the end. Odds are, you'll improve the passage, too.

☐ **Elevate your awareness of pacing.** When two characters plan to ruin somebody's marriage and sit around drinks talking about how to set up the tricks and traps of their plot, you know you can ease off on word length and allow a few more passive constructions. When a couple gets into a dogfight, you know you must tighten the action. This REI tool acts as a guide. Once again, you can measure progress.

☐ **Explore word choices.** When words like *dependability* and *extrapolations* grind your scores into the dust, you will find precise, short words. Or else you will cut the monsters from the page.

☐ **Identify detours and asides.** When either the writer or a character flies off on a tangent, this tool will shine a light on the sin. Once you see it, you can fix it.

☐ **Manage word count.** I don't know if you have this problem, but when I rewrite, I always blow the word count off the charts. To me, editing means adding. Improving means filling in blanks. But with this tool, I tend to fix things, not fatten them. You'll have to try it to see if it affects you the same way.

☐ **Write with economy on first drafts.** This might be the best effect of all. The pain and shame of seeing how fat my early drafts are make me want to write leaner prose the first time around. I can already see the improvement in my writing.

☐ **Create distinctive characters.** On second thought, this is the best effect of all. You can apply the scan to various charac-

ters and allow the college professors and lawyers in your stories to speak at a better readability level. But the kid from an
East L.A. gang isn't going to have the same score. (Is she?)

If your word processor doesn't have a readability test, no problem. Millions of computers do have them, and you can carry
your novel around on disk looking for one to rent or borrow.
It's worth the effort.

CAUTIONS ON RUNNING THE REI

1. **Do not run a reading ease scan on your entire novel at once.**
   The software will give you overall readability statistics but
   you will find them a waste of time. Entire sections of your
   fiction might be boring dreck full of passive constructions
   and a readability at the Ph.D. level. These might be followed with crisp scenes of high-energy dialogue and fast
   action. The two might average out to meet the ideal standards you set for yourself, but the dreck will earn rejec-
   tions for you. So work with one scene at a time. Set a standard
   that depends on the importance of the scene and the energy level you wished to achieve, and edit your work either
   to meet or exceed that standard.

2. **Evaluate your own favorite writers in the type of fiction you
   plan to publish.** My chosen writers and their novels came
   from different genres and varying literary acclaim. You might
   select two novels apiece by five romance writers, if you plan
   to sell romances. Or you might choose five thrillers by the
   same author. Just make sure they are best-sellers. Scan their
   work. Use the results to set a standard for yourself. I'm not
   saying you should copy another writer. Just that you should
   adopt the tools of his success to your own fiction.

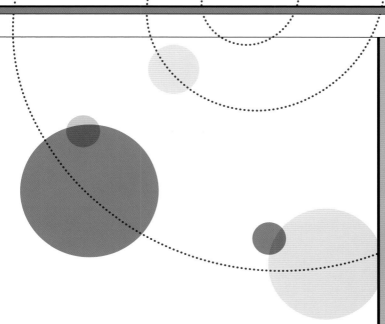

3. **Create a master file of the original version of your fiction.** Do this before you work your editing magic on a copy. That way if you cut too deeply you can refer to the master copy and restore selections.

4. **Turn off spell checks and grammar checks.** Do so, except for the feature that checks passive constructions. That way the scan will work faster.

5. **Create a log and enter your results each time you edit and rerun your own scan.** That way you'll be able to chart your progress with each version and make needed adjustments.

6. **Above all, don't rely on readability and mathematical results alone.** Use all the standard editing tips you learned in school, on the job, from your own research, and from writing seminars.

THE *creative* WRITER'S BRACKETING TOOL

Remember, back on page 98, finding creative words to fill in the blank for:

Thin as a _____.

Impossible as it sounds, let's find more words. But this time, we'll shoot for quality and variety, finding high quality answers by the prompts in this tool. I've filled in a couple blanks to show you how:

AUTOMATIC	thin as a rail (a stick, a broom stick, twig, whip)
OBVIOUS	dime
COMMONPLACE	_____

LITERAL	one millimeter
LABORED	_____
INTERESTING	_____
UNUSUAL	_____
OBSCURE	_____
ODD	beaver tail, rattlesnake
OPPOSITE	_____
INVENTIVE	_____
CREATIVE	_____
MAGICAL	_____
AMUSING (THE GRIN VARIETY)	_____
AMUSING (BELLY-LAUGH VARIETY)	_____
AMUSING (SLAPSTICK VARIETY)	_____
OUTRAGEOUS	_____
RIDICULOUS	_____
OBSCENE	_____
PREPOSTEROUS	_____
OVER THE TOP	Thin as Australia

WORD CHOICE

Here are my solutions:

AUTOMATIC—thin as a stick (a broom stick, twig, whip)

OBVIOUS—thin as a dime

COMMONPLACE—thin as paper

LITERAL—one millimeter thin

LABORED—thin as the space between two rails of a railroad track

INTERESTING—thin as dish water

UNUSUAL—thin as a railroad tie

OBSCURE—thin as a two-micron garbage bag

ODD—thin as a beaver tail, rattlesnake, dictionary, headstone

OPPOSITE—thin as molasses (rhinoceros skin, crocodile skin)

INVENTIVE—thin as vinegar

CREATIVE—thin as e-mail

MAGICAL—thin as angel skin

AMUSING (THE GRIN VARIETY)—thin as a television plot

AMUSING (BELLY-LAUGH VARIETY)—thin as day-old roadkill

AMUSING (SLAPSTICK VARIETY)—thin as month-old roadkill

OUTRAGEOUS—thin as a Rush Limbaugh's skin

RIDICULOUS—thin as mud

OBSCENE—thin as baby urine

PREPOSTEROUS—thin as a Stephen King novel

OVER THE TOP—thin as Austria (and you thought Australia was stupid)

How did I do?

If you'd like to argue with my responses, go ahead. I don't blame you for thinking that none of my answers in the Amusing category is all that amusing. But you must understand once again that this creativity tool doesn't evaluate right or wrong. Rather, it helps you strike a creative spark.

TIP: You can set up a scale of your own in the Bracketing Tool. Just replace my adjectives with useful gradations that fit better with your genre or line of work. You might choose terms like: business, spiritual, biblical, journalistic, poetic, musical, math-related, academic, scientific, gibberish. Whatever moves your creativity quotient.

DIALOGUE

exercise

WHAT ARE THE KEYS TO WRITING GREAT DIALOGUE?

Let's edit this bad dialogue to discover what good dialogue is.

"I'm leaving now," Wilma stated.

"I wonder if you should go at all," her mother countered.

"You're not going! And that's all there is to it," her father said angrily.

Wilma argued, "I've made up my mind, and you can't stop me."

"Oh, dear," said her mother. She began rocking ever quicker and quicker in her rocking chair, unable to decide whether anything she might say could change her daughter's mind without sending her husband over the edge.

Her father moved to the doorway and declared, "Over my dead body." He folded his arms. He stood looking squarely at Wilma, taking a deep breath, standing up on his toes to make himself look bigger, daring her to try anything physical.

Wilma walked across the room and stood before him. "Good-bye, Father."

"Good-bye, Wilma." He stood aside.

"I love you both," she said. Then she was gone.

> "I'm leaving now," Wilma stated.

Change to:

> "I'm leaving now," Wilma said.

Said is an invisible word. Any other word breaks the rhythm.

> "I wonder if you should go at all," her mother countered.

Change to:

> "Don't," her mother said. "Please."

If you use strong words inside quotes, then you don't find yourself straining to help out in the narrative. Notice how the fix tells us something about the meekness of the mother, too.

> "You're not going! And that's all there is to it," her father said angrily.

Change to:

> "You're not going and that's all there is to it," her father said.

No exclamation point. Never use punctuation in place of strong words. It's a lame attempt to prop up weak language. Same with the adverb, *angrily*.

> Wilma snorted, "I've made up my mind, and you can't stop me."

Change to:

> "I've made up my mind, and you can't stop me."

You can't grin, sneer, chuckle, or snort words. Also, the context inside the quotes tells us who's speaking. No need to repeat it with attribution.

DIALOGUE

> "Oh, dear," said her mother. She began rocking ever
> quicker and quicker in her rocking chair, unable to
> decide whether anything she might say could change
> her daughter's mind without sending her husband
> over the edge.

Change to:

> "Oh, dear," said her mother.

Get rid of the clutter.

> Her father moved to the doorway and declared, "Over
> my dead body." He folded his arms. He stood looking
> squarely at Wilma, taking a deep breath, standing up on
> his toes to make himself look bigger, daring her to try
> anything physical.

Change to:

> Her father blocked the doorway. "Over my dead body."

So much clutter. Besides, the scene should emphasize Wilma
more than her father. After all, once her father blocked the
doorway, who else inside the room would say those words?

RULE OF THUMB: When one character acts or thinks in the same paragraph as a segment of dialogue, there's no need to attribute. Your readers
will assume that the character speaks the line.

> Wilma walked across the room and stood before him.
> "Good-bye, Father."

Change to:

> Wilma walked across the room and stood before him,
> chin thrust at his chest.

We have reached the moment of truth in this scene, the confrontation between father and daughter. Words inside quotes aren't necessary when body language will do.

> "Good-bye, Wilma." He stood aside.

Change to:

> He folded his arms and stood looking squarely at Wilma,
> taking a deep breath, standing up on his toes to make
> himself look bigger.
>
> She raised her head and stared into the eyes that
> dared her to take him on. She did, but not in the way he
> could have withstood her, not physically. She simply
> enveloped his eyes in hers and touched his soul. He surrendered in stages, first blinking, then dropping his
> head to break her grip on him. He swallowed hard, wavered, and stood aside.

I wrote longer to make a point. In the original, the change in attitude was too sudden and not motivated. At the climax of the scene, for no apparent reason, the father gave up.

The revision gives you an image of silent confrontation—again, no dialogue. Finally, and more believably, he gives in to Wilma. The correction allows a reader to take a pause as the action plays out subliminally—during a logical pause in the dialogue exchange.

Leaving the final line alone.

> "I love you both," she said. Then she was gone.

DIALOGUE

marketing YOUR OWN SERIES

WHAT IS ESSENTIAL WHEN INVENTING YOUR OWN GENRE SERIES?

1. **Invent a killer series title.** Indicate the audience, the level of action or emotion, and the category. If possible, strike a familiar chord. The first book in my "Delta Force" series, written under the pen name John Harriman, is called *Delta Force*. Followers of military fiction don't need more than those two words to know what this book is about. (Refer to page 190 for title tips.)

2. **Come up with a subtitle that complements the title.** If you already have a killer title, you may not need a subtitle. But the *Delta Force* package title does need one precisely because it is part of a series. The subtitle is: *Operation Michael's Sword.* My publisher marketed the second book under the title: "*Prelude to War*, the second explosive book in the Delta Force series." In other words, if you liked the first book, here's a new title that continues the "Delta Force" series.

3. **Write a one-paragraph overview of the concept.** Describe the category in which the series will be placed and distinguish it from all other series in the category.

4. **Add a detailed overview.** One or two pages, double-spaced. In my own case of proposing the series, each character in the cast got a sentence or two of elaboration. A discussion of weapons, enemies, operating instructions, and general ground rules then followed.

5. **Write a sizzling summary paragraph.** Self-promoting or not, I give you the words from the back cover of *Delta Force*:

> Delta Force is America's elite, a highly covert counter-terrorism team that can carry out surgical strikes anywhere in the world at a moment's notice. But the one scenario that eluded them was a terror attack on American soil (on 9/11). Now Delta Force must … hit back at America's enemies with a wrath from which there is no sanctuary.

6. **Include a procedural page.** Write a list of conventions for each story in your package. This allows an editor and agent to understand the limits and procedures under which a story will play out. Take vampire stories. In some stories a necklace of garlic keeps the blood suckers away. They operate only at night. They avoid mirrors. Fly like bats. Sleep in coffins. All of these are rules or conventions.

7. **Show the format your story will take.** Or more to the point, story formula, which is not a bad word in packages. This segment sets down rough structure that all stories within the package must conform to: the opening incident, the villainous force, the quest or mission, the launch of action, setbacks along the way, final resolution, and redemption. Like that.

8. **Write brief character dossiers.** One page max for each of the major continuing characters in your package. These pages

work best if they look something like a résumé, not a full biography. You simply reveal the headlines of the character's life, especially those things in a person's past that can give clues about her personality. You might cover: special skills, role in the story, age, personality, physical description, background, and pertinent data like religion, language skills, hobbies. You might have as few as six or as many as ten characters you want to highlight in this way. Fewer than six characters suggests you might not have enough substance for a package. More than ten risks boring the editor or agent with too much detail. Even if you have thirty superb characters, limit this part of the package to the six or eight best.

9. **Tell some rousing story lines.** Or plots. Consider developing a dozen story situations and describe each on a half-page. (Here's a chance to use that Ten-Scene Tool on page 6 to huge effect.) Don't get into subplots, repetition of material that appeared earlier in the proposal, or extrava-

gant developments in characters. In keeping with the format you already described, tell what's going to happen—in about one hundred words—in a collection of exciting dramatic stories. Fewer than ten story situations might indicate you haven't given enough thought to the series. Or that your material is too thin to sustain the package. More than a dozen story lines is simply overkill. And remember, these plots must sizzle.

10. **Write your author bio.** More than anything else, you have to establish that you can complete a package that you begin. This is where writers with established credits will have an edge on the beginner, especially if they have already completed novels within a series.

11. **Offer follow-up materials.** You can take care of this in your sales letter to the editor or agent. Established novelists proposing a new package can offer to send published books as writing samples. Beginners can offer sample chapters, but I would recommend being prepared to send the entire first novel of a new series.

In fact even established novelists should have ten thousand words or so already written. Not that you have to prove you can write. Your published materials should establish that. But you do have to give editors and agents a taste of the characters, plots, and the tone of the package you're proposing. Not to mention that it will give them a feel for the quality and quantity you can deliver.

That's the package, twenty to thirty pages packed with promise. And a writing sample ready to send upon request showing that you can deliver on that promise.

DON'T GO
INTO THE
basement

WARNING: Don't allow your characters to do stupid things.

In a story where the screen is literally bathed in blood after a series of basement murders, why would any story's character, after hearing a strange noise, open the door, call out, "Who's there?" and go on down?

And why does a brilliant, competent lady cop rush into a fight against half a dozen black-hat, black-belt bruisers without even calling first for backup? Don't these people in the movies ever go to the movies?

Don't blame the character. Blame the writer. He wants to pit the character against the enemy *mano a mano* (or often enough, *womano a mano*), so he turns good people stupid and throws them into the fray. The lesson?

Don't position characters in terrible situations simply to let them demonstrate qualities like heroism, toughness, sensitivity, or any other quality for that matter. The artifice shows through every time and weakens your story.

When you pull a stunt like that, readers don't like it. And if you treat readers like dopes, they get the last word. They can shut you down by shutting your book.

So anytime a character encounters a terrible situation, the predicament ought to have been logically foreshadowed as an outcome of previous events. No matter what choice a character makes under duress, a reader should be able to conclude without straining credulity that the character has proven himself capable of that decision by his actions in previous, less stressful situations or by his nature, which the writer already has at least hinted at.

Having said all that, I add a caveat:

Don't rule out illogical behaviors.

CHARACTER

The huge mistakes that fictional characters make contribute to the very best stories of our times. If Ishmael had heeded a fortune teller's warning not to go aboard a whaling vessel, you'd have had no Moby-Dick to vex him at sea and you in school. Without Woodrow Call's itch to drive a cattle herd to Montana, an entire cast would have lived boring lives in the town of Lonesome Dove, dying of alcohol-related diseases or in drunk-riding accidents.

the **ACIIIDS TEST** *for evaluating scenes*

The ACIIIDS test will help you focus your writing as you go and evaluate your scenes after you've finished a first draft. You wouldn't want to give equal weight to each element in a scene, would you? No. Focus on one. In a drama, the irony scene might be much shorter than a scene that is primarily action. Put your scenes to the ACIIIDS test before and after writing so you prevent that writing from being scattered by the attempt to do too many things. Again, when in doubt, split a scene into two or more scenes, each with its own focus.

THE ACIIIDS TEST

ACTION—the level of movement or activity in a scene

CONFLICT—the level of argument or contention in a scene

IMAGERY—the level of visual cues in a scene

INVENTION—the level of creativity in a scene

IRONY—the level of wit, or sense of humor, in a scene

DIALOGUE—the level of conversation in a scene

SUSPENSE—the level of tension in a scene

I argue that every important scene must contain each of these elements. Further, one of those elements should dominate the scene.

ACIIIDS INTENSITY SCALE: ELEMENT TO EMPHASIZE
(Circle one):

Then mark each scale with the intensity of
each element in the scene (at its peak):

ACTION	impending	incidental	overt	urgent	frenetic
CONFLICT	tension	passive-aggressive	open hostility	injurious	fatal
IMAGERY	suggested	incidental	telling	active	determinate
INVENTION	cheap trick	blink-blink	wondrous smile	expletive	WOW!
IRONY	subtle	dry/sarcastic	visual	laugh	take your breath away
DIALOGUE	internal	monologue	debate	argument	imbroglio
SUSPENSE	invisible	subtle	cheap	chapter show	awesome	nail-biter

Using the intensity table on the scene card (on page 89), evaluate your scene, element by element. Circle the level of intensity you find for each of the seven elements. Which one dominates? Is it the element you intended? Use this tool as a guide as you edit. Revise to punch up elements you want to emphasize.

more EDITING HIP SHOTS *and* QUICK TIPS

Before you send your writing sample, check for these items.

BE CAREFUL OF THESE MISTAKES

☐ *Their* is possessive. *It's their car.* *They're* is the contraction of *they are. They're going to collect their revenge. There* is the pronoun, as in *over there.*

☐ Don't modify *unique* with *very, more, rather* or *so*—*unique* is *unique*, one of a kind.

☐ Don't use *anxious* when you mean *eager. She was anxious to collect her lottery winnings* suggests that she was worried that somebody, perhaps the IRS, might try to take it from her. I'm thinking *she was eager to collect her winnings and even more eager to spend it.* Memory aid: *anxious* refers to *anxiety.*

☐ *Currently* means *now*; write *now. At this point in time,* put simply, also means *now.*

☐ Don't string nouns together as adjectives. As in *emergency procedure qualification flights.* What the writer meant was *check rides.*

- *Catastrophic mishap* really means *crash*. By the way, *accident* usually means *crash*, too.

- Watch out for *activity*. It's often a sneak-attack of redundancy. It's not a *sports activity*; it's a *sport*. *Thunderstorm activity* is one or more storms.

- *Advance plan?* Why not a simple *plan?* After all, isn't the notion of advance preparation included in the four-letter word *plan*? Same with *future planning*. (And in any case, what good is *retro-planning*?)

- *Rather?* Avoid using it as a qualifier. *Rather pretty?* Not unless you mean Dan the former news man. Avoid *very* as a qualifier, too. Writers use *very* and *rather* because they're too lazy to look up a precise word. *Rather* sounds pompous besides.

- You *center on*, not *center around*.

- *By the same token,* say it if you like, but never write it in your fiction.

- Don't use parentheses. (Do as I say, not as I do.)

- *Criterion* is singular, *criteria* refers to more than one criterion. Same deal with *media*. It's *the media are jackals*.

- *Quality* is a noun, not an adjective. A *quality product*? No, a *high-quality product*. Or low.

- *A joint collaboration* is a redundant collaboration. Or perhaps the sharing of an illegal substance.

THE *ultimate* PACING TOOL

When you go to reader reviews on Amazon.com, the one comment you find most often when a lot of readers like a book has to do with pace: *I couldn't put it down. I stayed up all night reading. A real page-turner. The story was over so fast. What happened to the time? I missed my train stop.*

Like that. It's called pacing.

> *Every good novelist knows how to pump up the action in high-energy scenes. Every bestselling writer has an instinct for building pace, then letting off on the gas, then racing to the finish of a novel.*

If that's what you'd like to achieve, this tool's for you.

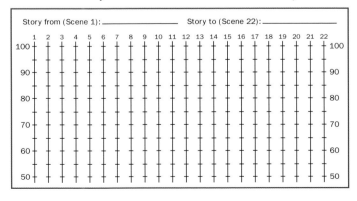

{152}

Here's how to use the Pacing Tool to measure the pace of your novel in 22-scene segments or fewer.

1. Use your word processing program to give you reading ease stats for your first scene in a 22-scene segment. In the *Story from* blank, write a word or two to remind you what's in this first scene where you're starting to measure pace in this segment of your novel. In the *Story to* blank put a reminder to yourself about what's in the last scene you measure.

2. Edit the first scene now if you like, until it meets all five goals of the Reading Ease Ideal (see page 66 or 68) for the word processing program you use. Or just go to the next step to see how you did on the draft you've written ...

3. Figure the REI composite for the scene. *In MS Word*, you subtract the Flesch-Kincaid level from the Flesch Readability score to arrive at the composite for your scene. *In WordPerfect*, you add the sentence complexity to the vocabulary complexity and subtract that result from 100 to get a composite. Either composite will work on the Pacing Scale.

4. Place a dot on the vertical line for scene 1 at the height that matches your score. In the example on the following page, you'll see a score of 70 for scene 1, a 72 for scene 2, a 74 for scene 3, and so on.

5. Evaluate each scene and get a composite for each, all the way across the scale.

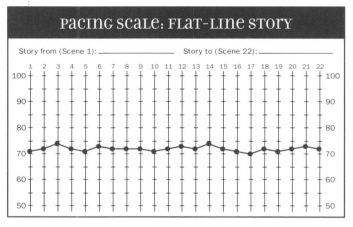

PACING SCALE: FLAT-LINE STORY

Story from (Scene 1): _____ Story to (Scene 22): _____

6. Connect the dots as I have done in green in the example figure.

7. Hold the figure at arm's length. What you see is a visual representation of the pace of that 22-scene segment.

8. Marvel at the coolness of your new discovery, but …

9. Be a bit concerned that the line is so flat, then …

10. Relax. We can fix that. Just wait until you get to Adjusting the Pace of Your Novel on page 194.

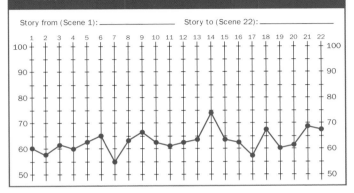

PACING SCALE: A LOW-INTENSITY STORY

Story from (Scene 1): _____   Story to (Scene 22): _____

11. Observe. Here's a second possible outcome to your graphing. In contrast to the flat line story, see how the graph above shows a good variety of pace from lows to highs and a general sense of rising pace to a climactic moment in places. That's a good thing. It shows excellent pacing instincts in the variety from scene to scene. The problem is, overall, the pace of the story is below 65 on the REI. The pace never rises as high as it could if the author went to work tuning his fiction in every scene.

12. Relax. That problem, too, can be fixed in the editing process. We'll learn how to retain the variety of pace and lift the overall pace of a story in the Adjusting the Pace of Your Novel segment on page 194.

PACING

{155}

CONFLICT IN
dialogue

The very best-selling novels are full of conflict, and nowhere is that spice better used than in dialogue. Characters should never just talk to pass the time of day. Fictional people should argue on some level, nay, on all levels. Let me count the levels:

Overt aggressiveness. Action or language that inflicts or threatens some form of abuse.

> She pulled a stun gun and pointed it. "One more step, and you're a break-dancer."

Passive aggressiveness. A far more interesting form of hostility, in which a seemingly submissive character can wreak havoc on a dominant one.

> She set the casserole on the table. Gray chunks floated up in steaming chartreuse sauce. "Tuna and beet goulash," Mother Parker said.
> "I hate beets."
> "Oh, really? Randall says it's your favorite."

Provocation. When one party taunts or dares another.

> "Ron," he said. "You have to confront her now. If you don't, she won't stop calling you."

Undercurrents. Conflict remains beneath the surface.

> He raised his glass. "A toast to our undying love." He said it without so much as a smile.

Ambiguity. The reader and characters might not be able to decide if conflict is actually taking place beneath the surface. Only the writer knows for sure.

> He poured. "Taste this Zin. It's to die for."

If a later scene reveals the truth of that declaration, the ambiguity is revealed and resolved.

Subliminal conflict. The characters engage in what they think is innocent banter. Readers know that disaster looms right around the bend. You know what I'm talking about. Every horror movie in existence uses this technique.

Word choice. Clipped Anglo-Saxon words can suggest conflict. All the best curse words in English derive their power from the Anglo-Saxon sounds.

Compare this:

> "Would you appreciate having your patella impacted by my podiatric appendage?"

With this:

> "How would you like me to kick your kneecap?"

Sentence length. Abrupt sentences elevate conflict. Same with strings of abrupt sentences.

Contrast this:

> "I don't like your attitude and if you don't apologize—and promptly—I'm afraid we'll have to stop seeing each other."

To this:

> "I don't like your attitude. Apologize. Now. Or else we're through."

{157}

Paragraphing. Short paragraphs suggests higher emotions, if only because readers read them faster. Higher emotions hint at conflict. Combining short paragraphs and short sentences can increase the effect. Read the previous example, then this:

> "I don't like your attitude."
>
> He looked down.
>
> "Apologize."
>
> He studied his nails.
>
> "Now."
>
> He found something to gnaw at on one finger.
>
> "Or else we're through."
>
> He sighed and held out the finger to her. "I need an emergency manicure, don't you think?"

Rhythm. Rearranging words can suggest conflict, especially if you create snap at the ends of sentences and paragraphs.

Compare:

> "Listen when I'm talking to you."

To:

> "When I talk, you listen."

Repetition. Key phrases add emphasis when repeated. Be wary of doing this one to death.

> "When I talk, you listen and listen good."

Using the affirmative. Which of the following suggests a higher level of conflict?

> "I'm not kidding."

Or:

> "I'm serious."

Using the imperative. This adds emphasis to the most neutral statements, as well as increasing the potential for conflict. Notice the difference between:

> "I don't think you should tell her the truth."

And:

> "Don't tell her the truth. Lie. Lie your tail off."

Typographical emphasis. Do NOT rely on this "AMATEURISH" technique!!!!

Body language. Overt actions and passive behaviors indicate conflict.

> "I don't exactly hate you," she said, blinking with only one eye.

Character recognition. Neither the author nor the narrator gives away the hostility. But one character sees conflict in an otherwise innocent situation. By saying so he tips off everybody else.

> "You say you've forgiven me but I can see the muscle cramps in your temples."

{159}

story STRUCTURE

the conventional story model

Most writing how-to books will tell you that stories are comprised of beginnings, middles, and endings. I agree, more or less, and used this figure in my workshops for years.

the master story model

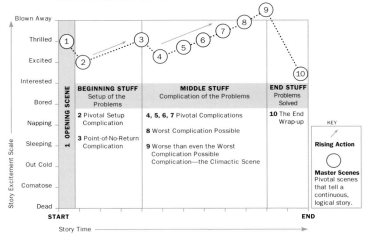

The way I see it, a story has four discrete, critical parts. These are:

- **Opening Scene:** Your *Opening (1)*, in my opinion, has to be the second most influential scene in your story, after the climax. That puts it in a class by itself.

- **Beginning Stuff:** *Setup Complication (2)*, with action rising to the *Point-of-No-Return Complication (3)*.

- **Middle Stuff:** *Complications (4) (5) (6) (7)*, the *Worst Complication Possible (8)*, with action rising to the *Climactic Scene (9)*.

- **End Stuff:** *Wrap-up (10)*, including the ending, epilogues, and the like.

RULE OF THUMB: Write your opening scene with the idea that it will persuade an editor to ask to see your completed work of fiction. Write your climactic scene (and the complications along the way) with the notion that it will make the editor's buying decision.

So that's the conventional story model. If it works for you, use it. If you want to lift your vision to a less conventional model, visit the Triumph vs. Tragedy model on page 204.

Everytime my computer has ever crashed
in the middle of writing an unsaved scene
and I had to rewrite it all from word one,
it's turned out better.

*There's a lesson in that,
and I think it's this:*

*I don't need a muse;
I need a less
dependable computer.*

THE
alternative
TO
description

Learn to write powerful images. Here's a tool to help.

ADVANCED IMAGERY VIDEO EXERCISE

1. **Rent a video that has been adapted from a published novel.**
   Then find the novel and a published screenplay of the same
   story. Choose something in the genre that you want to write
   your fiction in. *One True Thing* will appeal if you want to
   write about dramatic family relationships, for example.

2. **Review the video.** Look for one important scene in each of
   the following categories:

   a. A silent scene. Choose a powerful scene without dialogue. Make sure it involves a major character. If you have
   chosen a movie adapted from a novel, find that scene
   within the novel, too.

   b. A scene of dialogue. Choose a powerful scene in which
   two characters argue.

c. An action scene involving major characters and dramatic physical play. No need for car chases or gun battles. Even if the actors merely storm around the room pointing fingers and scowling, that's action enough. Once again, find it in the novel if you can.

3. **Novelize the silent scene.** Watch the pictures on film and re-create those images in writing. Try to be brief, accurate, and active. The great thing about this exercise is that you don't have to invent images out of whole cloth. You won't even be searching your memory banks to recall an experience of your own. You don't even have to rely on a static photograph or picture of the setting. Once your imagination is freed from having to invent or recall events, you can concentrate on simply creating the image in words as it appears to you onscreen. When you're finished novelizing, make the following comparisons:

a. See how the screenwriter handled this scene. Of your novelization, the original author's published version, and the screenplay, the film script is likely to be briefest. The screenplay uses shorthand terms to describe the elements that the writer must convey to the director and cinematographer. Did you identify the same aspects in your own image?

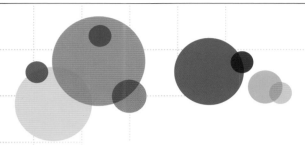

b. Compare your version to the original author's.
Did the screenwriter and the author agree? And did your
descriptions fall into line with the author's intent?

4. Novelize the scene of dialogue in the video. Follow these
steps:

a. Capture the spoken lines. Transcribe the actor's
lines, word for word from the film, not the novel or the
screenplay. Use only a minimum of attribution or none
at all. If three or more people are talking, or if both are
of the same gender, use a modified script technique
such as:

Sam: "I don't understand you, Diane."
Norm (butting in): "Why not?"
Sam: "This is insane."
Diane: "No, you're insane."

To get the most out of this exercise, transcribe at least two or
three pages of dialogue exchanges. Then …

b. Rewind the video to the beginning of the scene.
Mute the volume. Now observe closely.

c. Play the scene without sound. Watch for action that
accompanies the language in the dialogue you have cap-
tured. Notice emotions and other images supplied by

the actors. Examine telling images going on in the background of the primary action. Pay attention to elements on film that the director and cinematographer highlighted by lighting, camera angle, focus, cuts, close-up, and other techniques. Take notes.

d. Rewind and play back the scene. Do this as many times as necessary as you write only the essential narration. Observe images. Capture those images in words and supply the lines an author might write between sections of dialogue. You needn't write half a novel to get the benefit of this exercise. In fact it's better if you stick to a minimalist approach. Don't interfere with the continuity of the dialogue.

e. Compare. Take your final product and compare it to both the screenwriter and the original author.

5. Finally, perform the same exercise on the action scene. Begin with a transcription of pure dialogue as you did in the last exercise. Then create action and images from what you see onscreen with the volume on. Action scenes often require noisy sound effects. Dialogue might not be the most essential element within the scene. So the images you create will be often more violent and more sensory.

When you have finished, make the same comparisons as before. The screenwriter might well have written half a page or more describing the action that will take place in high-intensity moments of his film. And the original author might devote many pages to suspenseful scenes.

This exercise, even if it requires you to write several thousand words of work you can never publish as your own, will be valuable experience in your personal writing development.

GRABBING
the
READER

THE FIRST 100 WORDS

An editor or agent might read a thousand words before decid-
ing to either reject your work or to ask for the full manuscript.
But you can't afford to waste a single word of the first 100 words
because those words will help create your:

FIRST IMPRESSION AT THE BOOKSTORE

You might not have much to say about your book's title, cover,
preview quotes, or ad copy that pitches your novel. But any
potential book buyer who has been motivated by those things
to pick up your novel will glance at the first paragraph or two
to get a taste of your storytelling ability. Those first 100 words
must snag his interest and hold him like a Velcro-captured
cotton ball so that the only time he dares relax his grip on your
novel will be to lay it on the counter to get out his wallet.

A CHECKLIST FOR THE FIRST 100 WORDS

This critical segment of the work must, at a minimum:

☐ Set the tone of the narrative, including vocabulary, attitude, and harmony of language

☐ Establish a point of view

☐ Preview the mechanics of the story, including sentence length and density of paragraphs

☐ Sketch in a suggestion of the setting

☐ Hit the reader between the eyes with an element of *Oh wow!* at some point in those first 100 words of your writing

A tall order.

Test this observation about the first 100 words by picking up any novel, script, or play. Count words. (If the hundredth word falls in the middle of paragraph, include the entire paragraph in your sample. This gives the writer a fair chance to finish her thought.) Evaluate the material according to the helper's checklist. You could learn a lot from this little exercise.

CAUTION: Don't press too hard with these opening words. Just as in trying to meet somebody you admire, it's possible to go breathless and appear needy if you try to hard. You'll be tempted to overwrite an overwrought opener if you're not careful. Be cool. Be natural. No matter how hard you have to work at it, make it look easy.

WHAT
striking
words
CAN DO

USE STRIKING WORDS TO:

☐ **Create a powerful sensory image.** In John Grisham's *The Street Lawyer*, you'll find these words in the first paragraph:

> I didn't see him at first. I smelled him though ...

☐ **Open an emotional vein.** Kaye Gibbons did this in *Ellen Foster:*

> When I was little I would think of ways to kill my daddy. I would figure out this or that way and run it down through my head until it got easy.
>
>   The way I liked best was letting go a poisonous spider in his bed. It would bite him and he'd be dead and swollen up and I would shudder to find him so. ...

- **Jolt the reader with a sense of dissonance.** In Terry McMillan's *How Stella Got Her Groove Back* you find:

  > ... much as I loved my son, I was glad to see him disappear.

- **Capitalize on the outrageous.** Make sure, however, that you always remain wary of being too gimmicky. In Nora Roberts's *Montana Sky,* this is the opening sentence:

  > Being dead didn't make Jack Mercy less of a son of a bitch.

- **Shape a fresh language impression.** Jay McInerney in *Bright Lights, Big City:*

  > ... you rode past that moment on a comet trail of white powder ...

- **Tantalize with a sense of drama, irony, or suspense.** Winston Groom's narrator, Forrest Gump, says:

  > Probly, tho, I'm closer to bein a imbecile or maybe even a moron, but personally, I'd rather think of mysef as like a halfwit, or somethin—an not no idiot ...

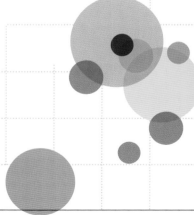

PROPOSING *the* "BIG BOOK"

HOW CAN I TELL WHETHER I HAVE THE RIGHT
STUFF FOR A POTENTIAL BLOCKBUSTER NOVEL?

THE ELEMENTS OF A "BIG BOOK"

Besides strong writing and magical stories, a big book requires:

A category-like handle. Courtroom thriller. Coming-of-age story. Political murder mystery. Romantic thriller. Medieval saga. Improbable love story. Women's adventure. Psycho thriller. Offbeat spy novel. A story for Oprah.

Be wary of the word *thriller*. Everybody loves a thriller. I think you could invent a unique big-book idea for a novel just by connecting any word to thriller. Western thriller. Computer thriller. Classroom thriller. Medical thriller. Legislative thriller. Thriller thriller. Publishing thriller.

You must write adrenaline-pumping action and suspense from the very first pages of your novel to live up to that thriller billing.

Showbiz tweak. By this I mean a phrase that jogs the imagination. Even if it's a bit hokey, something that performs two important functions:

One, it connects your idea to the world of Hollywood, Broadway, high-profile celebrity, sports, politics, pop culture, or even the classics.

Two, it tells what your story's about.

Use the first line of your query letter to tweak an editor's interest by writing:

> In my near-future war novel, *Jurassic Park* meets World
> War III as genetic weapons threaten to wipe out human-
> kind.

All you're doing with this eye candy is getting attention in a shorthand way. Editors and agents talk to each other in such telegraphic language all the time. If you were to overhear the "let's do lunch" chatter you'd likely hear editors and agents using terms like:

> "Batman is on Hannibal Lecter's dinner menu."

> "The war in Iraq revisits *Cold Mountain*."

> "Cosmo Kramer runs for president."

From this point on, you must stop trying to sell sizzle and begin to deliver substance.

Captivating major characters. I can't think of any classic novel or film whose blockbuster success could not be attributed in great part to dazzling characters, great and small. Characters rich and realistic. Characters quirky and complex. Characters demonic, or at least dark. Characters that the audience feels honored to have met in fiction or too frightened to ever meet in reality. Or both.

No matter how good or evil, these characters must connect with readers of your fiction. People must wish that they themselves could be as heroic as your heroic characters. They must see in those characters things they fear finding in themselves, even in the good guys. They must applaud when the character overcomes these awful flaws within themselves in order to achieve whatever plot quest you have set for them. Readers must also find moments of compassion for your villains. Hannibal Lecter has that soft-spoken sensitive side. You find yourself sympathizing with him, a serial killer and a cannibal. That can't be healthy for you, even for a moment. But it is a remarkable quality when you can evoke such a feeling in your own fiction.

Distinctive minor characters. Nobody is ordinary in big-book fiction or blockbuster film. Think about *Shakespeare in Love.* Everybody in the film was somebody. The minor characters came to life. But they did even more than live. We saw them as people with goals and interests and opinions. They each had an effect, however minor, on the story. The really big stories always have big-little people.

A dominant issue with a twist. The dominant issue dictates the overall personal stories of individual characters. The example that swims to the surface first in my mind is *Schindler's List.* The Holocaust and all its horrors occupied center stage on screen, overshadowing yet another huge theme, World War II. Nothing happened in the film unless it was caused by the Holocaust or its perpetrators and victims. That's a big issue to end all prominent issues.

The power to stun. In *The Western Canon* (Harcourt Brace), Harold Bloom writes:

> One mark of ... originality ... for a literary work is a strangeness that we either never altogether assimilate, or that becomes such a given that we are blinded to its idiosyncrasies. Dante is the largest instance of the first possibility, and Shakespeare, the overwhelming example of the second. Walt Whitman, always contradictory, partakes of both sides of the paradox.

This notion fascinates me for two reasons. One, all my favorite stories have this quality of weirdness. *The Catcher in the Rye*, *M*A*S*H*, *A Clockwork Orange*, *Lonesome Dove*, *Fargo*, *Ulysses*, *One Flew Over the Cuckoo's Nest*, *Angle of Repose*, *August 1914*, *Andersonville*, *Seinfeld*, *All in the Family*, *The Monk*, *The Detective*, *Treasure of the Sierra Madre*, *Apocalypse Now*, *Avalon*, *Pulp Fiction*, *Homicide*, *American Beauty*, almost anything Elmore Leonard—you get the idea and have your own list.

Two, because the line between strange and over-the-top is so tricky that only the very best sense of balance permits a writer to walk it.

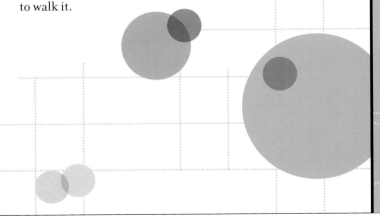

NAMES

CHECKLIST FOR NAMING CHARACTERS

☐ **Brainstorm a list of names before you begin your novel.** Collect last names for every letter of the alphabet. Use a phone book, almanac, or *The Writer's Digest Character Naming Sourcebook*. Then build lists of male and female names—one or two first names for each letter. With this list at your fingertips, you don't have to stop your story to name a new character that bursts into the tale. You can just pick a name, put it on a character card (seen on page 53), and keep on keeping on.

☐ **Don't use names of real people.** If you name a character after your sister, and then that character flies out of control in your story and kills everybody at the Post Office, how are you going to feel? You'd have to stop the novel and re-name her, right? Or else be prepared never to talk to your sister again.

☐ **Avoid names that begin with the same letter.** Betty, Brandi, Briana, Bobby, Bud? Bad idea because too many such names can be confused with each other.

☐ **Avoid names that can be both male and female.** Pat, Terry, Kelly, Les, Robin, and a boy named Sue? Unless your story confuses the identity to create a twist.

- **Be wary of first last names.** Grant or Tyler or James or Chase. Each name could be last or first. I'm not saying not to use them; I'm saying that if you do use them, do so knowingly, so you can deal with the ambiguity.

- **Don't overuse alliteration — first and last names beginning with the same letter.** Alice Adams, René Rousseau, and Melanie McManus in the same story? Too much.

- **Don't use names that sound like half the people in the phone book.** Mary Jones? Bill Johnson? Nuh-uh. Try to be a little creative. And never use Jim Smith — it's way too common already.

- **And don't use names that rhyme in the same story.** Think Mary, Carrie, Barry, Gary, Perry, and Zarrie (Zarrie?). Too much confusion. And too cute besides.

- **Be wary of long names.** Typing them can kill you and building macros can too. And readers get bewildered.

- **Be conscious of names ending in -s.** This can cause awkward punctuation when you want to show possession. Suppose your heroic character is Regis Jones. Whatever he possesses is Regis's. When two or more members of his family appear in a scene, they are the Joneses. Their house is the Joneses' — enough to make you avoid such names altogether.

- **Don't be cute.** I.M Boring? Okay, if that's how you want to come off to your readers.

- **Don't use a name twice.** Remember. Cross a name off your list when you name a character.

paragraphs
THAT
sing

Writing effective paragraphs requires that you apply many of the same principles you use with sentences and words, such as keep them short, simple, and focused. I must amplify the notion of singularity (focusing on one central idea), which is larger with paragraphs.

Paragraph singularity means keeping to a single topic in a single paragraph. It also refers to a consistent attitude, a single direction, and unity of focus. As you might guess, a well-written paragraph also uses a variety of sentence forms in varying lengths. And one paragraph is often tied to other paragraphs in scenes and stories with the use of tie-backs and transitions.

Don't worry that I'm about to launch into a grammar lesson. I think the best way to deal with all these features is to give you:

YOUR PARAGRAPHING CHECKLIST

Paragraph Length

☐ Evaluate your paragraphs for length. I don't prescribe paragraph lengths, but you ought to be aware if they go on too long or if they're all too uniform. When paragraphs are all the same length, a sense of monotony sets in.

☐ Vary paragraph length by one or more elements of action, conflict, imagery, irony, or dialogue.

☐ As you boost action, conflict, and dialogue, you'll often find yourself writing shorter sentences and paragraphs. The problem will take care of itself.

Paragraph Density

☐ Hold your manuscript at arm's length and go through a scene one page at a time. Do you see any white space on the page? If you're writing one paragraph on each page, the story looks gray, feels gray. Probably is gray.

☐ Can you use dialogue to break up the huge blocks of type just by adding white space? That's a trick that helps move a story along.

☐ Can you juice up a boring paragraph just by adding a few carriage returns or some quote marks here and there?

☐ If the material is boring in huge blocks, it'll be boring in small bites, too. But all other things being equal, adding some breaks can relieve the gray.

WRITING
SCENES *with*
IMPACT

WHAT IS S GOOD WAY TO CREATE IMPACT
IN A SCENE?

Take your story from one scene to another without dallying.

The term *smash cut*, comes from film writers. It implies a jarring, abrupt scene change. For instance, the closing shot in one scene might be a beautiful woman sipping her coffee as the red sun rises over the mountains. Smash cut to the red fireball of an ear-splitting explosion over the mountainous landscape of a city skyline. Get it?

The fiction writer's smash cut can save a lot of miles in writing transition and explanation of how a character got from one place to the other. The best way to illustrate this is by example.

A chapter's ending sentence:

> He was so proud of himself and couldn't wait to hear what Mama would say when he told her what he had done.

Followed by a page break and the opening of a new chapter with:

> "You imbecile," Mama said. "You scant-wit, slack-jawed, mouth-breathing, knuckle-dragging idiot."

Nothing but the turn of a page stands between the character's wondering what Mama will say and what Mama actually says. No taxi ride. No bus transfer. No subway graffiti. Not even a description of how a proud son broke the news to his incredulous mother. The writer assumed that you could assume anything you wanted between his wondering and her reacting. The result is a pro result.

Any other way to create impact?

Best-selling authors often achieve a powerful effect by skipping over the action and showing the result, a technique similar to the smash cut.

> "I told you not to talk to me like that, Randy," she said.
>
> "I told you what I was going to do if you talked to me like that again."
>
> He blew a stream of air between his lower lip and upper teeth. "Get me a brew."
>
> "What did you say?"
>
> "You deaf? I said get off your butt and get me—"
>
> He cradled his nose in his hands, huffing blood through his fingers.
>
> "See?" she said, standing over him, her fist still balled. "See what you made me do?"

No wind up, no punch, just the punch's effect.

ADVANCED

imagery

TECHNIQUES

WHAT ARE SOME TECHNIQUES FOR WRITING GREAT IMAGERY?

I groan every time I read this writing advice or any of its clones: "Employ accurate description to enrich your writing." You might as well tell a sculptor to use sharp chisels. Don't write description. Rather than describe, create powerful images.

Replace labored descriptions with a single image:

> The ice-fog distracted him with its sparkle, its glitter, its dazzle. It was like a shower of shimmering, weightless particles of glass.

Becomes:

> The ice fog glittered like a dust storm of glass.

We used nouns and verbs instead of adjectives. *Glittered* includes all the notions of *sparkle*, *shimmer*, and *dazzle*. One sentence replaces two.

Replace strings of microscopic details with one small but telling image. Note how *a dust storm of glass* doesn't need to be clarified as a *shower of shimmering and weightless particles* anymore. And notice how a glass storm suggests an element of danger, which may come into play later.

Set static situations into motion as dynamic sensory images.

> He felt like a kid again.

A statement by the author, now becomes:

> He opened his mouth to collect the particles. He couldn't feel them, but he could taste them. And surprise, they tasted like dirt.

Use precise verbs and concrete nouns in the active voice. And a peculiar jolt of finding that an ice-palace scene tastes like dirt. Now instead of the ice fog distracting him as it would a child, he's doing things that affect his senses, just as a kid would (and without saying so). Which allows us to …

Emphasize character awareness over author awareness.

> He should have known better than to dally in the cold while he was still a mile away from camp.

This might be the narrator speaking, but as it stands now, without context, the voice sounds like the author chiding the character-treating him like a kid, in fact. It's an easy fix:

> He was still a mile away from camp. And, sure, they told him not to dally.

What does this change have to do with imagery? Written this way, the passage confirms character awareness. It emphasizes the sensory effects of preceding images. And it sets up the punch line to have more punch because you'll read how the

{183}

character experienced the action and imagery rather than how the author reported the experience.

Weave images into the action and conflict.

> But he fooled around until the sun came, bringing him to his senses. He shielded his eyes with one hand and set off toward camp, but before he'd gone even half a mile he could see nothing but dazzling, dancing spots. Snow-blind.

If you read the original versions of this example in order, you get a feeling of: *So this looked like that. Then the other happened. Then another thing happened. Until finally the guy was blind.* The scene feels like an unpolished first draft. You could correct that feeling by skipping from the word *dally* to the next segment.

Above all, don't overwrite imagery. Avoid images that stand in the way of action, conflict, and dialogue.

Nothing distracts a reader more than stopping a story's momentum to describe. In the next example, I'll exaggerate the egregious sin: interrupting dialogue.

> She found him kneeling on the trail.
>
> "Ross?" she called to him, breaking into an awkward hippety-hop run through the knee-deep snow. "Are you all right?"
>
> He straightened up and tried to get to his feet, but he was trapped, waist-deep in a snowdrift, a low wall that had begun to drift to his shoulders. "Sara? Is that you?"

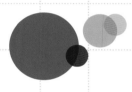

Becomes:

> She found him kneeling on the trail in a waist-deep
> drift, his fists pressed into his eyes.
>> "Ross?" she called. "Are you all right?"
>> "Sara? Is that you?"

Two things. One, let your people talk. Two, don't belabor a point by endlessly recasting an image. No need to trip up both characters in snowdrifts.

Try cutting imagery altogether. Have you ever considered eliminating passages altogether in your writing? Using the hidden text feature of your word processor, eliminate a selection. Do you find anything missing between the previous scene and the successive scene? If you can revise either with a few transitional words, consider that the intervening passage could be left out. Ask yourself whether you'd like to keep it, but only because there's a personal gem of writing in it that you cannot live without. I suggest having it both ways. Delete the passage from your text and save it in a separate file for later. Maybe you can use it in the current piece of fiction. Or maybe in your next novel.

My agent once made a deep impression on me in a discussion about *The Bonfire of the Vanities*. She said, "Sometimes I wish Tom Wolfe wouldn't describe so much, and in such excruciating detail. Sometimes I wish he'd just leave a little bit to my own imagination."

Best advice about imagery I've ever gotten.

FOCUS

HOW CAN I STAY FOCUSED ON MY STORY?

Here's a tool to help you from the very start.

THE NUGGET

In forty words or so, write down what your story is about. Here's an example from one of my own tales, written under the pen name of John Harriman:

> *Delta Force*
>
> A Military Thriller
>
> A soldier watches the 9/11 terrorist strikes on the Twin Towers from an airliner. The mission: Train a hit squad to exact revenge without becoming American terrorists in the eyes of the world. The risk: Losing his own soul.

That's thirty-nine words, not counting title and category. I wrote it at the very start of writing the novel. I shared it with my editor to let him know my focus. I kept it on hand to remind myself whenever the story felt as if it were foundering.

HOW TO KEEP FOCUS USING THE NUGGET

☐ Type or hand-print your idea onto three-by-five cards.

☐ Carry one in the pocket of your blouse or shirt.

☐ Put one in the place where you'll be writing your novel. Put another on the visor of your car.

☐ Carry one in your planner.

☐ Keep this Nugget before you as a reminder of your novel and the story you have committed to telling.

☐ Anytime you feel you're drifting from the story you set out to write, you can do one of two things:

> Thing One: Get back on track.
>
> Thing Two: Write another nugget that describes your new focus.

VOICE

ALL MY CHARACTERS SOUND ALIKE.
HOW CAN I MAKE THEM DISTINCTIVE?

Use this ...

DISTINCTIVE VOICE TOOL

To help you remember this tool of voice, I've identified five qualities, all beginning with the same letter as voice.

Vocabulary. Word choices made by the character. Pet phrases. General vocabulary level. Give your characters distinctive words. Give the character her own vocabulary.

Verbosity. On a scale of brevity to verbose. You can create a distinctive voice just by controlling the length of a character's thoughts and speeches. Give this trait attention for each character.

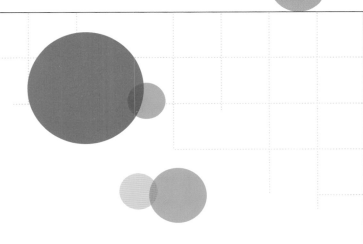

Velocity. The pace and rhythm of a character's speech and thoughts. How you arrange words, sentences, and ideas. Each character gets her own pace.

Viewpoint. In two senses. First the overall attitude toward elements and characters in the story. Second the literal point of view and omniscience allowed that character by the author.

Venom. Emotional intensity and the capacity for swings in mood. Make each character definitively toxic.

Use this tool to identify qualities you can jot down in your notes about your character (refer to the character card on page 53). You can establish distinctive voices for every character in your novel. Then, when your character comes into a scene after having been absent for fifty pages or so, you can refresh your memory about what makes him unique.

If you do this well enough, a reader will be able to distinguish characters by their speech alone. When that happens, you've arrived as a writer.

TITLES

The first words a publishing professional or consumer audience will see about your work almost certainly will include the title words. If your novel, play, or film is remembered at all, that title will be the handle by which everyone carries its memory. Most important, titles sell. Even so, no matter how you cut it, a great title is of no value without a great story behind it.

QUALITIES OF TITLES

A great title is endowed with the elements of this checklist:

☐ **Stopping power.** Usually meaning it is short and snappy. One to three words. You could name a thousand exceptions. Even so, between multi-word best-selling titles like *Midnight in the Garden of Good and Evil* and *Divine Secrets of the Ya-Ya Sisterhood,* you will find hundreds of three-word titles. Until a publishing professional examines your story in full and passes judgment on its greatness, be brief. Think in publisher's terms. A short title lends itself to ease of handling in reviews, advertising copy, and cover typography. One or two words can be printed larger on the cover or poster than fourteen. Examples:

> *Cheaters*
> *Hannibal*
> *The Edge*

❑ **An ability to position the work.** This is especially important in category fiction, if that's what you're writing. A selection of a title should indicate whether the intended readership is primarily men or women. Beyond that, is this novel a Western, a romance, a science-fiction tale, or what?

> *Dangerous Kiss*
>
> *Hannibal*
>
> *The Girls' Guide to Hunting and Fishing* (Not that this novel is so much a guide to the outdoors, but that it's a title that makes an open, if ironic, appeal to women.)

❑ **Word images that suggest cover art.** Does your title conjure a picture that ought to go on the cover? For instance, do you remember the image on the cover and ad copy of *Jaws*? *Jurassic Park*? *The Silence of the Lambs*? Of course you do. (Jaws, T-rex bones, and death's head moth, right?)

❑ **Simplicity and directness.** It is usually not obscure, bizarre, or made up. Once again, you can find dozens of exceptions. Just remember, you're selling. You wouldn't intentionally write an advertisement for a spot during the Super Bowl that might cost a million dollars that did not tell viewers the product you were trying to peddle. Granted, an obscure title might not prevent a first reader from checking out the first line of your synopsis to find out the topic of your novel. But why make a mystery of it?

conflict:
THE
INDISPENSABLE
ELEMENT
IN FICTION

CAN I WRITE A STORY WITHOUT CONFLICT?

Good luck. Do you care that nobody will read it? Nobody in the reading or listening world, let alone the publishing industry, is going to pay any attention to your work, let alone pay money for it.

> *Conflict sells. More so than sex, which in all its forms and treatments usually can be condensed into conflict anyhow.*

I doubt you can name any title or category in commercial fiction in any medium that is not bound up, so to speak, with conflict. Conflict occurs in:

- **The most wholesome family shows:** *Father Knows Best*
- **Animated features:** *Cinderella, Tarzan, The Lion King*, you name it
- **Obscenity-free fiction:** anything by Jan Karon or Danielle Steel
- **Children's stories:** anything Harry Potter
- **The Bible:** everywhere from Genesis to Apocalypse

In a word, everywhere.

You see, hostility, violence, and strife aren't by themselves objectionable in fiction. True, some forms of writing glorify such things and even worse things. But that's not what I'm saying here. I'm saying two things:

Thing One: Good characters can't be interesting unless they triumph over something, normally an evil thing. This involves conflict. The stronger the conflict, the more precious the victory. It's one of the more fundamental facts of life.

Thing Two: One of the best places to exploit conflict is in dialogue exchanges.

adjusting
THE PACE
OF YOUR NOVEL

HOW can I Get THe most From THe pacing scale?

Remember the two examples of stories that show up as poorly paced in the segment, "The Ultimate Pacing Tool"? Here they are again.

In this first example, you measured the pace of a story and found it level. That story will drone unless you fix it.

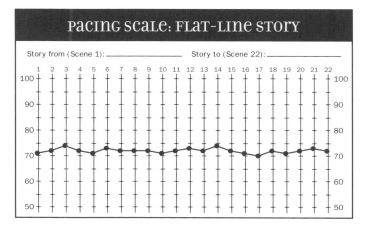

PACING SCALE: FLAT-LINE STORY

Story from (Scene 1): _____ Story to (Scene 22): _____

In this second example, you found a good variety in the stories pace, from highs to lows, but overall most of the story ran below the Reading Ease Ideal.

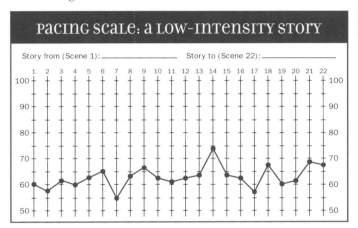

PACING SCALE: A LOW-INTENSITY STORY

Story from (Scene 1): _____   Story to (Scene 22): _____

Both problems can be fixed when you edit strategically using the five goals of the Reading Ease Ideal and this tool. Use the Pacing Scale in two ways.

way one

Evaluate the 22-scene segment purely from a graphic point of view. Is it flat, more or less, all the way across the segment? That's not good. Even if your pace is fast, the lack of variety will tire a reader and force you to press to keep it up so high. At a glance you know the pace of this segment in the novel needs variety. Pick the spots where you'd like to slow the action and edit those scenes. You might use the passive voice, longer sentences, and bigger words in an existing scene. Or you might write a more leisurely scene and insert it into the story. Or you might pick spots to elevate.

Or you might even decide the whole profile is low and elevate all of it, particularly in strategic spots like scenes 11 and 20. In which case, you'd want to refer to …

WAY TWO

Evaluate the 22-scene segment from a content point of view. Over the course of that part of the novel, did you intend to write a number of scenes with high energy? Identify these strategic spots on the graph. For argument, let's say scenes 11 and 20 in our example are major confrontations between your heroic and villainous characters. You know those must read at a faster pace than you've achieved so far. Circle the spots where you threw your characters into such conflict, where the action should race along, but does not.

Now you know where to edit for a faster pace.

> *Remember, the quickest way to pick up the pace in a scene is to cut. Cut long sentences down to size. Cut long words from the piece. Use short words instead. Cut the passive voice to 0 percent. Use simple, declarative sentences, active voice, short paragraphs.*

RULE OF THUMB: You get the fastest pace in a high-energy scene when the scene averages ten words per sentence, a max of four characters per word in MS Word (one syllable per word in WordPerfect), and 0 percent passive sentence constructions.

When you have key scenes that absolutely, positively must read faster, set this higher Reading Ease Ideal, mentioned in the Rule of Thumb, for yourself and see what happens as you edit until you reach it.

Finally, as you rewrite and edit the entire 22-scene segment a second time, plot your results again, this time in a different color, as I have done in this example.

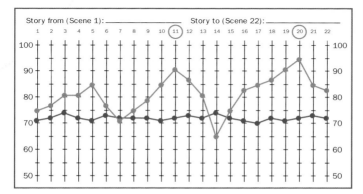

Now that looks like a segment of a novel with some variety in pace, doesn't it? And across the board, a faster pace altogether.

What's very hot in this tool is your new ability to hit a fast pace in strategic scenes in your fiction.

CHARACTER
redemption

WHAT IS THIS NOTION OF REDEMPTION IN A NOVEL?

Every major character in a story ought to have a chance at redemption. Your audience should recognize that moment of redemption. Your character should recognize the moment, even if it has passed and can't be had, even if it is offered and refused, often to huge dramatic effect.

YOUR REDEMPTION CHECKLIST

The notion of redemption literally includes words like:

- [ ] To recover
- [ ] To set free
- [ ] To buy back
- [ ] To atone
- [ ] To avenge
- [ ] To reward good deeds
- [ ] To punish bad deeds

To those literal meanings I'd add these literary ideas:

- [ ] To know
- [ ] To be aware (the epiphany)
- [ ] To see error
- [ ] To correct error (resolution)
- [ ] To know the difference between right and wrong
- [ ] To vow to do better from now on
- [ ] To be better
- [ ] And, if no form of redemption applies, at least to be witty, which we have come to know as the Hollywood wisecrack at the moment of death and destruction

Let's see how some fictional characters have gotten their redemption. The easy ones first. Hamlet avenges his father's killing at a high cost. Lear sees the error of his ways and at least dies reconciled to the one daughter true to him. Robert Urich's character in *Lonesome Dove* is hanged, but at least he's sorry. Harrison Ford's character in *The Fugitive* proves his innocence— and Tommy Lee Jones's character proves he believes in that innocence. These are so easy. The Lone Ranger always puts things right and rides off with a Heigh-ho, yadda, yadda, yadda.

Let's look at two tougher cases. Hannibal Lecter escapes to eat again in *The Silence of the Lambs*. That's redemption for him but leaves us feeling a little queasy. He's smart, witty, and capable of compassion. But he's got the eating disorder to end all disorders. Macbeth, one of the bloodiest killers in literature, would rather die like a man than yield to a life of ridicule.

As a rule, nearly all Hollywood and most category fiction—romance, horror, action, Western, mystery—redeem characters in the endings. The bad guy is punished. The good girl gets the guy. The poor get rich, and the rich get poor. Mainstream fiction often leaves the issue of redemption ambiguous.

> *No matter what you write,*
> *offer redemption.*
> *Then let the character accept*
> *or reject it.*

I find this rejection the most powerful option of all. I don't mean those stories where the bad guy, who deserves to be killed, gets his just desserts to the raves of the audience. No, I mean a character, either heroic or anti-heroic, sees redemption at his grasp. He decides to forego it (or he decides not to decide, which loses it for him).

> *Dramatically speaking, these situations—when characters can have redemption but turn their back on it—give us our best dramatic pieces.*

The Nazi officer Amon Goeth, played by Ralph Fiennes in *Schindler's List*, might have had partial redemption just by pardoning Jews instead of killing them—although he'd already killed so many. Macbeth considered sparing his king and enjoying his titled status and universal respect. But he went for the gold instead, using a killing spree to win the crown.

In *Fargo*, the smiling villain, Jerry Lundegard, played by William H. Macy, might have called off the scheme to kidnap his wife at any time before the two thugs broke in on her. With a simple phone call, he could have met her for lunch and saved her life. He could have admitted to the crime at almost any time before the kidnapper killed his wife. The combination of his greed, his desperation, his ignorance, his cowardice, and his stupidity caused any number of deaths in this film, a tragedy worthy of Shakespeare.

And all because a character refused to redeem himself.

Never show your writing
to anybody who doesn't love you enoug[h]
to tell you when it stinks.

Oh, and anybody who tells you,
"It's nice, dear,"
is really saying,
"It stinks, dear."

TRIUMPH
versus
TRAGEDY

Here's a new way to look at story structure, a little helper I invented for my own use because, for better or worse, I try to tell stories as if they were films. It's a combination of traditional story models and the Ten-Scene Tool (as seen on page 6).

First the model.

TRIUMPH VS. TRAGEDY STRUCTURE

ACT I	ACT II	ACT III

Triumph
Tragedy

PONRC *

Climactic Payoff *
& REDEMPTION

My Big Fat Opening *

YIKES! Moment *

Up-Tick & Reversal *

Status
Quo

Up-Tick & Reversal *

ICGAWTT Moment *

OYICRB Moment *

Money Shot Moments *

Now the explanation.

Triumph is your goal in this story model. The top dotted line shows the boundary between triumph and tragedy. I look at the story as a journey toward triumph, a tale told in terms of one tragedy after another.

The Status Quo. The second dotted line is a status that only exists before my story begins because I try to open big. Thus …

My Big Fat Opening. A film developer once told me that when she reads a script, the first thing she's really looking for is, "Are you freaking me out by page three?" If you think about it, that's the way films go. It's what I alluded to in my Master Story Model with the Opener (see page 160). I call this the first Money Shot in the story, a scene of utter importance along the journey to triumph. After the opening, the story might or might not return to a temporary status quo until the …

PONRC. This is the Point-of-No-Return Complication. The moment at which nothing can ever return to the status quo.

Up-Ticks & Reversals. Call them complications if you like. The heroic character will see some progress in his quest of a worthy goal, then suffer a setback. Each setback will be worse than the last. The hero will continue to fight bravely. The setbacks will continue to knock him down a tragic path until the …

ICGAWTT Moment. It-Can't-Get-Any-Worse-Than-This Moment. Followed by the …

OYICRB Moment. Oh-Yes-It-Can, Rock-Bottom Moment. Where all hope of recovery is certainly lost. How dark this moment can be and how difficult it is to overcome are the measures of great story. But naturally, the hero does overcome and rockets toward triumph, his flight set back once more by the …

Yikes! Moment. At which the hero must overcome one last surprising obstacle before achieving …

Climactic Payoff and Redemption. Try sketching your novel into each of the eight moments. I have found this a useful tool. I hope it works as well for you.

In most ways this model is no different from any other three-act format to describe story structure. Except. In three ways, it's a true whack on the side of the head with a two-by-four.

First, it gives a writer no room to establish a status quo, no static situation, no setup. The status quo is assumed. It happened before the action, before the first crisis, ahead of the Big Fat Opening.

From the moment of the opening that freaks you out, it's a model of a story in motion. It's a tale with a direction. It's a story with momentum. It's always headed toward tragedy, always full of tension in the struggle toward triumph. The only times things return to the status quo are in those brief moments of passing through, downward on the way to tragedy, and upward on the way to triumph.

Second, the model gives a writer some milestones to hit along the way from beginning to end. I may know from the first what my Closer, or climactic moment will be. But the model

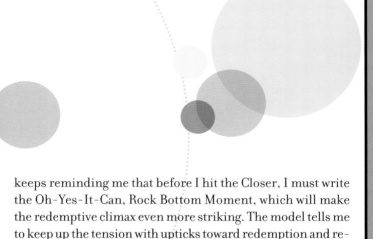

keeps reminding me that before I hit the Closer, I must write the Oh-Yes-It-Can, Rock Bottom Moment, which will make the redemptive climax even more striking. The model tells me to keep up the tension with upticks toward redemption and reversals that pave the way to tragedy. Without these milestones, a story can become a droner.

Third, there's that ultimate story payoff, the Redemption above all. Whether the heroine achieves redemption or rejects it might not be decided, but I always keep it in mind that every dramatic story is made more dramatic by writing toward redemption. "Stay on track," the model reminds me. "Write the way to Redemption that follows a long road of tragedy."

This is more than a model, more than a roadmap to writing fiction. It's a target that gives me the final bull's-eye to shoot at and reminds me to address intermediate targets along the way.

EDITING SCENES
using the REI

Here's a tool for you to photocopy and use as you edit your fiction. It's a simple diagram with three blank charts showing the five measurements of the Reading Ease Ideal (see page 66 or 68 for more details). Choose the tool that matches your word processing program.

KEY: wps = words per sentence, spw = syllables per word.

REI EDITING TOOL (MS WORD)

Scene: _____

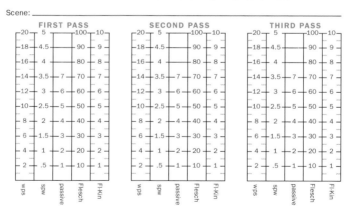

REI IDEAL FOR MS WORD

Words per sentence (avg): **15** maximum
Syllables per word (avg): **4.5** maximum
Passive voice: **5%** maximum

Flesch Reading Ease: **80%** maximum
Flesch-Kincaid Level: **6** maximum

Use this tool to evaluate each scene in your novel.

1. Run the Grammatik feature in WordPerfect or the Readability Statistics feature in MS Word on the highlighted scene.

2. Enter the results in the appropriate column.

3. Make a copy of the scene and edit your work in that copy until every one of the five areas meets the standard. Leave the original intact in case you have to recover cut material.

4. Chart your progress for each iteration of editing, making more photocopies of the charts if you need to.

5. After the scene meets all five standards of the REI, compare the edited version to the original. It should read smoother because the quality of your edited work is vastly improved.

REI EDITING TOOL (WP)

Scene: _____

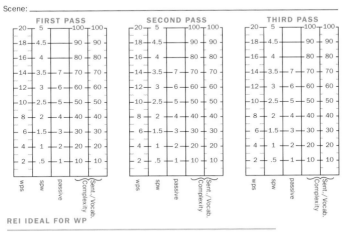

REI IDEAL FOR WP

Words per sentence (avg): **15** maximum   Sentence complexity: **30** maximum
Syllables per word (avg): **1.5** maximum   Vocabulary complexity: **15** maximum
Passive voice: **5%** maximum

GETTING
the reader
INVOLVED

HOW DOES A PRO USE POINT OF VIEW
FOR THE BEST EFFECT?

Do, don't tell.

Once in a while, if you keep your eyes open, you'll find an opportunity to exploit an interactive narrative device.

> One-thousand-one, one-thousand-two, one-thou-
> sand-three.
>
> He clenched his eyes and plugged his ears. Any sec-
> ond now. She should see the rubber snake.
>
> One-thousand-four.
>
> She should be screaming by now.

Rather than tell that the character counted to three, the narrator does the counting. Thus, the reader counts along with the character.

Here's a second example, from *Delta Force*, my book under the pen name John Harriman. In this segment of a much larger scene, one man is talking to a hospital patient who can't speak because of injuries. The injured man scribbles on a pad and uses common hand signs to get his half of the conversation across. The narrator interprets only very little, letting the reader decipher for himself. I edited the excerpt clarity and excised a few words to avoid giving away some plot points.

> "Couple things and I'll let you sleep," Spangler said.
>
> Baker flashed his palm. *What?*
>
> "Are you a Christian?"
>
> Baker scribbled. *No. Y?*
>
> "Muslim?"
>
> Thumb down.
>
> "Any religion?"
>
> Scribble. *Army—DF Army*
>
> "So, you'll do this?"
>
> Thumb up and fist clenched.
>
> "We changed your name. You're now Ramsay al Bakr."
> Spangler spelled it.
>
> Thumb up.
>
> "Second, I have a meeting to get to—you'll be happy to hear this—we're putting together a new team. ..."
>
> Open palm. *So what?* Thumb jerked toward the door.
> *Get lost.*

As you read this scene, you should feel as if you're participating in the deciphering of scribbles and hand signs. When you can, use a minimum of explanation. Trust in your readers to get the point.

PROLOGUES *and* EPILOGUES

SHOULD I use a prologue in my novel?

Don't. A prologue literally contains information that comes before the telling of the story, a kind of pre-beginning. As with forewords, dedications, acknowledgments, and credits, readers often skip them. So I recommend against prologues.

> *It's always best to start with the first piece of action that an audience needs on the path toward your ending. Don't spend dozens of pages setting up situations or establishing settings.*

Perhaps the most common amateur problem in writing fiction is the tendency to rely too much on setup. Which is what a prologue most often is.

Get on with story.

*Start in the middle of something,
with the action and conflict
already in progress.*

*When you do that,
readers like your material.*

*Stories take care of themselves
when they keep to a fast pace.*

WHAT ABOUT USING AN EPILOGUE IN MY NOVEL?

Depends. The word *epilogue* literally means an addition to the story. You shouldn't need one if you have delivered a satisfying ending to your story. Even so, I use epilogues frequently in writing category fiction where word limitations prevent me from creating a dozen or more scenes to tie up complications that can't be addressed in a fast-moving narrative. After a suspenseful climax, I prefer taking readers to the end of the story with a feeling of mission accomplished.

Readers do skip epilogues, but I figure, if somebody likes the book enough to get to the end of it, odds are good they'll at least peek at the epilogue. Besides, I always finish the central story before beginning an epilogue. I also leave at least one important mystery unsolved, and I unveil the solution in the epilogue.

But a final warning about using epilogues in the form of a personal story. My own daughter said she liked reading one of my books but couldn't figure out one unsolved mystery.

> "Are you going to take that up in your next book?" she asked.
>
> "The answer is in the epilogue," I said. "Didn't you read the epilogue?"
>
> "I never read that stuff."

Sob. My own daughter. So. I ask you: What can you expect from strangers?

If you decide to use an epilogue anyhow, try this checklist.

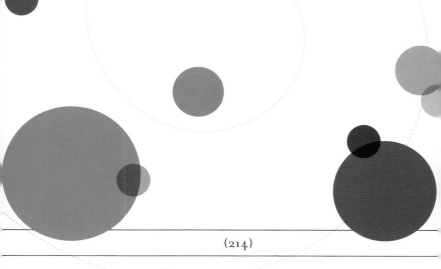

HOW TO HANDLE AN EPILOGUE

❏ Keep it brief. Don't exceed 1,000 words.

❏ Try using a checklist format, with short paragraphs and extra space between each. I often list characters and matter-of-factly tie up loose ends about unresolved issues for each of them.

❏ Don't try to address critical plot issues in the epilogue. You should satisfy yourself that, if they do stop reading your last regular chapter, they will have not missed anything of importance. Should you run up against an important unresolved issue, don't try to fix it in an epilogue. Go back and revise your central story, no matter how much rewriting you have to do.

❏ Don't get artsy-crafty with your epilogue. Speak to your audience like a narrator in a documentary. Just let them know what happened after the story ended.

❏ Don't take yourself or your work of fiction too seriously. Now is not the time to climb up on a soapbox and preach. If you haven't taught your lessons within the context of the story, anything you say after the story ended will have little value to your audience.

❏ Give your reader one last wisp of a smile or a gentle parting *Oh, wow!*

❏ Don't ramble on. Impart your after-story information, then: Stop!

TRANSITIONS

HOW can I make my novel FLOW smoothly?

Transitions. These come in two forms, large- and small-scale techniques.

SMALL-SCALE TRANSITIONS

Outright phrases. *Later, last week, next day, yesterday, then, soon after.* Like that.

Direct references. Often using pronouns like *he, she,* and *it* to refer to nouns in previous sentences and paragraphs.

Reflections of images and ideas. From one part of the scene to the next.

Repetition of words or synonyms. From one paragraph to another.

Cause and effect. Something happens in one paragraph, and its result is seen in the next.

Contradiction. Something is stated or supposed in one paragraph but is reversed in the next.

An overall dominant atmosphere to which references are made. This is tricky to talk about but easy to see. Suppose you set a scene at night in a black forest. From then on, any reference to darkness or blindness is a tie-back to that atmosphere. Cool, huh?

LARGE-SCALE TRANSITIONS AND TIE-BACKS

The really brilliant writer always keeps two notions at the top of his awareness. The first is simple cause and effect. The second is motivation. Both of these notions can be used to transition and tie back elements of a story.

Cause and effect. Something that happens in the present scene will result in something happening in a later scene. Perhaps nobody can say for sure what that effect will be. A good writer will have a number of possible consequences to create and sustain a feeling of suspense. She might achieve surprise by inventing a possibility that even the sharpest reader could not anticipate.

> *But by keeping to the fictional rule that actions cause reactions, the writer keeps the reader hooked. This feeling of suspense acts as an emotional form of transition.*

You feed a reader cause and effect often enough, and she will come to expect it. She will keep track of unsolved issues, waiting for you to spring your solution.

In the film *The Truman Show*, there is an early scene where Truman is outdoors and a rain shower is soaking him and only the space within an arm's reach around him. That scene hits you between the eyes because it's an image right out of the comics and cartoons. I didn't get the point of it at first because the larger context hadn't been revealed yet. When it did strike me later, it was a truly *Oh, wow!* moment. Of course, being a man-made world, the huge soundstage of *The Truman Show* was subject to the occasional glitch. Later, such glitches tipped off Truman to what was happening to him. But at the moment of that shower, neither he nor I understood what was going on.

Motivation. Motivation can be a second abstract transitional device. As you develop character, the reader begins to see what causes that character to tick.

> *As the reader begins to know and understand the character, he realizes that the events now happening in this fiction will, sooner or later, rub up against the individual motivation, which has a certain predictability to it.*

When that happens, and a character begins reacting, the reader expects to see certain semi-predictable responses.

It's an adage among playwrights that anytime a gun is introduced in the first act, somebody had better be shot with it before the curtain in the third act. The same can be said about cause and effect and motivation and response. You simply cannot put a madman's dynamite temper into play in the opening pages of your novel, light the fuse in the middle pages (carrying the reader ahead in the form of an abstract transition), and fail to provide an explosion in the climax.

As you write, you probably don't have to worry too far ahead about the simple transitions from word to word, sentence to sentence, paragraph to paragraph, scene to scene, and chapter to chapter. For any writer of modest talent, those things take care of themselves like the automatic body responses of heartbeat, digestion, and breathing. If you fall short in these areas, they are also easy to fix during the editing process.

STEREO*type*STEREO

HOW CAN I AVOID STEREOTYPES?

Simple. Acknowledge them. Exploit them. Make them distinctive stereotypes, if that's not too profound a contradiction in terms. First a few definitions.

TYPES OF STEREOTYPES

Stock characters. Ignorant southern redneck. Callous husband having an affair on the side. Know-it-all army officer (or know-it-all police department bureaucrat, academic dean, corporate vice president, parent, boyfriend, athlete, sorority sister—you name it, he or she knows it all). Drunken, brawling, bawling Irishman. Fashion-forward gay man who acts giddy. Butch lesbian woman with the acerbic wit able to put down any male character with a single quip. These are all stock characters.

Stock character behavior and reactions. Hostile minority member (whose reason for homicidal hostility is a past racial injustice). Pacifist goaded into a Rambo-like rampage. Beautiful, fun-loving prostitute with Jay Leno's wit and William F. Buckley's intellect. Anti-everything youth whose destructive, boorish behavior is ultimately put to good use in defeating a platoon of criminals and simultaneously solving all adult problems in a story.

Stock character situations. Boy meets girl; girl hates boy; boy and girl fall into bed; boy and girl fall out of love (although it has not yet been established that they were ever in love); boy and girl fall in love, after all, and live happily ever after. Arguably, this

stock situation occurs more often as a central story line or subplot in Hollywood films than any other.

Acknowledge these types. Then out of tired, worn characters, situations, and stories, create something fresh.

A SHORT GUIDE TO WORKING WITH STEREOTYPES

☐ Start with a stereotype character and change her in uncon-
ventional ways.

> *One way to do this would be to have the char-
> acter undergo a change in attitude and
> behavior over the course of the story. Unfor-
> tunately, this situation is all too common-
> place. Better to add extra dimensions to a
> character to transcend the stereotype.*

Perhaps the best example I can think of off the top of my head was Lieutenant Giardello in the old television show, *Homicide*. He could be demanding, unfair, and sometimes even on the far side of scrupulous in performing his job. In these aspects, he wasn't much different from any supervisor who ever tried to undermine Dirty Harry. But Giardello wasn't a one-dimensional character at all. He could show an entire range of emotions in a single scene. He was as loyal to his detectives as he was demanding of them. He was capable of a broad range of sensitivities. More often than being unfair, he was scrupulous. He failed to get a promotion to captain because he had been too honest in the past. Or not honest enough, depending on the other characters' point of view. In other words, Giardello was more than a realistic character—he was human, just like you.

☐ Use the stereotypes with only a few, telling modifications to type.

> *Let your audience know up front that even a one-dimensional character is capable of qualities that can be interesting. Each time a stereotype character, situation, or formula seems to resort to type, add a gentle twist to tweak the audience. In the end, capitalizing on both the predictability of a type and the unpredictability of view, the author creates a twist that might have been foreseen but was not.*

For instance, my Force Recon series came to me in the form of a bible from an editor who listed characters that might appear. One was Henry Friel, a kid forced from the streets of Boston to the Marines by a judge who offered him a choice, either to enlist or go to jail. He's a sharpshooter and wiseacre, a natural born killer. In other words, as one reviewer put it, a type. But a type that transcends even the stereotype in his own mind. You see, he knows he has a rep as a killer and acts up to sustain that image. But inside, he's torn by emotions that contradict type. As the novels proceed, we see that beneath the body of a cynic is the soul of any kid you've ever met.

writer's
BLOCK

WHAT IF YOU GET BLOCKED?

My take? Writer's block does not exist. It's just a form of laziness. Or distraction. Or, perhaps in the case of some true genius, a form of madness. But, as a rule, having been in magazine and newspaper journalism for much of my adult life, it is just a lame excuse to not write. I know, I know, people have written entire books on dealing with this ailment called writer's block. But I have a better idea for you.

Imagine yourself dressed in gown, mask, and surgical gloves standing in the center of an operating theater. By eavesdropping on the conversations from nurses and surgeons, you discover that you are the principal surgeon scheduled to transplant a brain from the picnic cooler beside you into the head of a dying patient. Your assistants have already peeled back the man's scalp and removed the half-dome of his skull. Everybody in the room begins staring at you expectantly.

"What are you people looking at?" you say.

Your chief assistant says, "It's time for you to transplant the brain."

You reply, "Maybe tomorrow. I can't find the motivation. Maybe I've got surgeon's block. What do you think?"

There's no such thing as surgeon's block. If the doctor doesn't do the operation after cracking that skull, it's because she's lost her nerve, lost her enthusiasm, or doesn't know what she's doing. Why do writers think they have the privilege of a special dispensation for not working? What is this mysterious white lie known as writer's block?

I've learned two things about creative writing. The first is that creativity doesn't strike sparks in you like a bolt from the ionosphere. You can't expect much from wandering around idyllic settings waiting for an inspiration.

> *The most effective aids to creativity continue to be a simple pen and a blank pad. You create sparks by striking one against the other. Write an idea down. Develop that idea. Turn the idea inside out. That's where creativity comes from.*

The second thing I've learned is that writing does not occur by thinking about it. Writing only happens when you do it, so plant your butt in a chair and get busy. Keep busy. After you create a million or so words, you will have established yourself as a serviceable writer simply from the experience. If you've worked hard at learning from your experiences along the way, you'll probably be a creative writer. That's how it works.

And by the time you've written those million words, you will have, like me, forgotten that the condition of writer's block even exists, except in the minds of dilettantes.

irony
IN DIALOGUE

How can I use irony without resorting to lame humor or smart-aleck quips you hear in action movies?

I confess I'm not the best person to ask about avoiding lame humor. But I like to read writers who don't take themselves too seriously and even allow their toughest characters to have a sense of humor.

Elmore Leonard in person must have a terrifically dry wit, judging from the number of characters in his books who are funny without cracking a smile.

Lee Child, in his novel *Echo Burning*, puts tough guy Jack Reacher into a hysterical situation without going slapstick. Reacher, trying to pass himself off as a ranch hand, is ordered to saddle a horse, but it's all he can do to figure out which way the saddle goes. Once he does, a young girl has to tell him to start over because he forgot to use a saddle blanket. Reacher is at his funniest when he has to remind himself that horses have hoofs, not feet. *Or is it hooves?* he wonders.

In *Delta Force*, a general at the hospital visiting a grievously hurt soldier feels sorry for the man's hideous face. While the in-jured man mocks the general, feeling lucky that he's not as ugly as the one-star. There's an irony in that. Right?

In my experience in an Army career, I found that men in the most exhaustive, trying, deadly situations can find some kind of dark humor. So even those Bruce Willis wisecracking moments at the brink of death aren't entirely implausible to me.

But your personal sense of humor will dictate the extent of the irony in your stories. It's not something you can spin out of whole cloth—if you try, the effort will show.

Even so, I'll give you three examples to illustrate ways to use irony which, from the overt to the subtle, act like an injection of adrenaline, pumping life into dialogue.

FICTION TECHNIQUES

Overt irony:

> "I'm such an idiot," she said.
> "Yes," he said. "You are."

Over the top (with apologies to Ring Lardner):

> "Are we lost, daddy?" I asked.
> "Shut up," he explained.

Subtle (I think):

> "I'm such an idiot," she said.
> He didn't answer.

Don't struggle with irony, but don't fight it, either. Don't be tempted to borrow from sitcoms or to tell jokes. Be aware enough to recognize that when a situation brings out a wry smile in you, it's worth trying capturing that smile to share it with readers.

SUBPLOTS

You can expect to find a romantic interest subplot in almost every kind of fiction. Family relationships. Career ups and downs. Love affairs on the side. Rebelling against authority. All or any of these themes might appear in your stories alongside the central conflict, as they do in many other stories.

But how to write them? In the truly brilliant stories, these are not tacked onto the main story line as if stuck on with stick-on notes. You know what I'm talking about. For the last two decades or so, nearly every film you can find has the obligatory sex scene thrown in. Or else the provocative instant in which some part of the anatomy, usually but not always female, is briefly exposed. And almost every one of those films could be shown, the scene excised, without damaging the central story line.

On the other hand, you find effective subplots woven into the fabric of the story part of a pattern that cannot be removed without shredding the main story.

> *If a subplot can be eliminated from a story without leaving a vacuum, likely it was tacked on, perhaps as a formulaic after-thought. The subplot shouldn't have been written in the first place.*

RULE OF THUMB: A subplot reveals itself to you as a natural outgrowth of the central action, the characters and their interactions, and from the everyday experiences of life. The subplot carries the audience forward toward the outcome of the central story by posing and solving intervening problems, always related problems.

Often, you can recognize that stock plot elements were plopped into movie scripts. Things like these story lines tend to be clichés.

SUBPLOTS TO AVOID

☐ The obligatory car chase, followed by ...

☐ The obligatory car crash, in which ...

☐ The bad guy gets away leading to the scene of ...

☐ Hatred-at-first-sight between hero and heroine, followed by ...

☐ The soft-focus sex scene between hero and heroine after a blow-up between them, followed by ...

☐ The lover's spat brought about by a misunderstanding that apparently ends the romance, followed by ...

☐ The lovers make up, usually with make-up sex, then ...

☐ They combine to defeat a legion of demons ...

☐ Leading to a love scene ...

☐ And so on, ad nauseam.

EXAMPLES OF SUBPLOTS

Nevertheless, here's a list, not exhaustive subplot material, using one of America's all-time favorite television shows, *Seinfeld,* as an example.

☐ **A continuing romantic interest.** For Jerry, one an episode, with a frequent reference to the past relationship with Elaine.

☐ **Personal quirks.** For George, repeated instances of his tendency to be a tightwad. And to be obsessed with parking spaces.

☐ **Personal graces.** The better angles of their nature. Like … gee, I can't think of anything right away. You read on. I'll think this over and catch up with you later.

☐ **Personal flaws.** The nasty, unpleasant angle—of a character's nature. Need I list them all?

☐ **Family relationships.** Jerry's and George's, for two that crop up every few episodes.

☐ **Mysteries.** Kramer's first name. Kramer's job. Kramer's dad.

☐ **Hobbies, careers, or technical interests.** Jerry as a stand-up comic. George's ambition to be a pretend architect. Kramer's creation of miniature art from pasta—art that appears in the background of the set in many an episode.

- **Job relationships.** Elaine's baffling relationship with a variety of bosses. George's continual boss battles.
- **Fears and deep, personal secrets.** Kramer's first name again. Jerry's unwillingness to commit to a woman. George's PIN number.
- **Personal history.** Past experiences that bear on the present situation. Cosmo's mother. The Jerry/Elaine relationship.
- **Talents.** Jeez, other than to make you laugh, do those characters have any?
- **The continuing effects of nature and the environment.** Big-city eccentrics and life, such as waiting "on line" form the backdrop of the series and play larger roles in many episodes.

You get the idea. Which is, as you can see from this illustration, that subplots, or situations in the sitcom, can often rise to enough importance to compete with or even become the central story. But they can also remain subliminal, occasionally cropping up to remind the reader that they are there.

FINAL EDITING
hip shots
AND
quick tips

Before you send your manuscript or writing sample, check for these items.

WORDS TO AVOID

☐ Avoid *however* in your writing. At all cost. *However* is hokey, even in fiction, however, even worse, it tempts you to string clauses together, making your writing bulky.

☐ Ditto *importantly* and *more importantly*.

☐ Ditto *in addition to* and *moreover*. Use the global search function of your word processor and cut these abominations from your fiction.

☐ *Prohibited altogether* isn't any more prohibited than *prohibited*. Just twice as long.

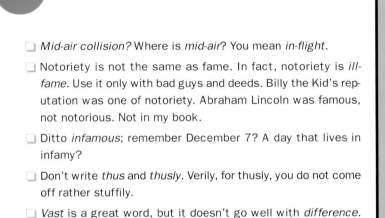

- *Mid-air collision?* Where is *mid-air?* You mean *in-flight.*
- Notoriety is not the same as fame. In fact, notoriety is *ill-fame.* Use it only with bad guys and deeds. Billy the Kid's reputation was one of notoriety. Abraham Lincoln was famous, not notorious. Not in my book.
- Ditto *infamous;* remember December 7? A day that lives in infamy?
- Don't write *thus* and *thusly.* Verily, for thusly, you do not come off rather stuffily.
- *Vast* is a great word, but it doesn't go well with *difference.* Because it sounds as if you're stretching the facts. Oh, and why not be the first writer in memory to write *wasteland* without the *vast?*
- *For the purpose of* has no purpose; say *to.*
- *End result?* No, *result.* The result of using *end result?* You don't sound as smart as you're trying to sound. Mentally, your readers correct you.
- Don't *commence, begin.* And for Pete's sake, don't *commence to begin.*
- Same with *proceed.* One best-selling novelist is fond of writing, *She proceeded to ask. ...* He means, *She asked.*

More things to watch for ...

ACCURATE WORD CHOICE

☐ Watch what you *make*, you could be making perfectly good verbs into cumbersome nouns. Don't *make corrections* to the report. Just *correct* it.

☐ Say *provide*, if you like, but write *give*.

☐ *Each and every?* Nah, pick one (not *one or the other*).

☐ It's *different from,* not *different than.*

☐ *Gather together?* Why not simply *gather?*

☐ *En route* is two words; it's not *enroute.*

☐ Don't use *individual* for person. And please don't write the redundant *one individual.*

☐ *If and when?* Use either *if* or *when.* And not *either/or,* please, pick one.

☐ *Whether or not?* Nope, just *whether.*

Watch your spelling too ...

COMMON SPELLING HANG-UPS

- [ ] *Accommodation* is a big word, so it takes two *c*s, two *m*s.

- [ ] *Alot?* Nope, you mean *a lot*.

- [ ] *Alright* is all wrong; you mean *all right*.

- [ ] Bizarre how many ways *bizarre* can be misspelled.

- [ ] *Embarrass*, with two *r*s but ... *harass* with one.

- [ ] *Judgement?* No, *judgment*—one *e*.

- [ ] *Occur* has two *c*s one *r*, and *occurred* has two *c*s and two *r*s.

- [ ] *Separate*, not *seperate*.

- [ ] *Souvenir*, not *souvenier*.

- [ ] *Receive*, not *recieve*; the rule is *i* before *e*, except after *c*. Yield; again, *i* before *e*, but *weird*, *e* before *i*. Weird, huh?

- [ ] Enough about spelling. Use the spell check.

THE *final* ULTIMATE PACING TOOL

Here's the best tool in your writer's tool kit, the most powerful little helper you'll ever find, the Binford 10,000 of writing tools.

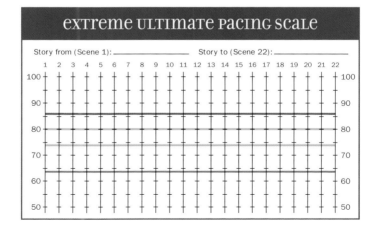

extreme ULTIMATE PACING SCALE

Story from (Scene 1): _____   Story to (Scene 22): _____

Okay, I admit it. This doesn't look a lot different from the first scale I gave you on page 150. Just four horizontal colored lines added to the pacing scale. But those lines are a way for you to keep track of pace instantly after you've subjected every scene to the Reading Ease Ideal goals and tight editing (page 66).

Let's talk about those lines.

Red Line. Breakneck pace: a composite REI of 86 or higher. On this line and above, your writing is at warp pace. My numbers come from the REI of MS Word, by the way, because I write in Word, but the same figure will translate in Word Perfect. If I'm writing a combat scene or a major personal conflict, I want the writing to be in this zone.

Orange Line. Thriller pace: a composite REI of 80 to 85. This is the pace of a thriller in a high-energy moment.

Green Line. Compelling pace: a composite REI of 74 to 79. This is the minimum range I'll accept in my writing. Except for an occasional dip above the …

Blue Line. A downshift in pace: a composite REI of 64 to 73. Once and rarely, twice, in a 22-scene segment of a novel, I'll let the action slow into this zone. Giving me a breather. And my characters. And my readers. But only for one scene in a blue moon, so to speak.

Remember, this tool uses composite numbers, which you learned to calculate on page 153.

last
WORDS

DOS AND DON'TS FOR THE LAST 10,000 WORDS OF YOUR STORY

☐ **Don't introduce any new characters or subplots.** Don't intro-duce anything new. Any appearances within the last fifty pages should have been foreshadowed earlier, even if mysteriously.

☐ **Don't describe, muse, explain, or philosophize.** In other words, keep the author out of the story, and don't let it drag. By this point in the story, setup is done, complication is wrap-ping up, and resolution should be entirely uncluttered so you and the reader can make an unimpeded dash to the finish line. Keep description to a minimum, action and conflict to the max.

☐ **Do create that sense of *Oh, wow!*** Once or twice on every page, if possible more frequently.

☐ **Do enmesh your reader deeply in the outcome of your story.** Make her unable to put down your novel to go to bed, to work, or even to the bathroom until she sees how it turns out.

THE FINAL 1,000 WORDS

In the last four to five pages ...

❏ **Resolve the central conflict.** In favor of the heroic character, if you please. You don't have to provide a happily-ever-after ending, but do try to uplift. Readers want to be uplifted, and editors try to give readers what they want. So should you.

❏ **Do surprise your reader.** Again, I'm not suggesting quirky *Twilight Zone* twists or trick endings. No "And then my alarm went off, waking me up" or "Why are you asking me? I'm just a dog" jerk-the-reader-around finishes. Nothing cute or stupid.

❏ **Afford redemption to your heroic characters.** No matter how many mistakes she has made along the way, allow the reader— and the character—to realize that, in the end, she has done the right thing.

❏ **Tie up loose ends of significance.** You don't have to establish a picture-perfect moment, that rare snapshot in time where every minor contentious issue is neatly solved. But every question you earlier planted in a reader's mind should be addressed, even if the answer is to suggest that a character will address that issue later, after the book ends.

❏ **Inject a note of irony, however mild.** Give your audience something to smile about, if only wryly.

❏ **Tie your final words to events in your Opener.** When you begin a journey of writing the novel, already having established a destination, it's much easier to make calculated detours, twists, and turns in your storytelling tactics. When you reach the ending, go back to insure some element in each of your complications will point to it. Such tie-backs don't require you to telegraph the finish. Merely create a feeling that the final words hearken to an earlier moment in the story.

❑ **Don't change voice, tone, or attitude.** An ending will feel tacked on if the voice of the narrator suddenly sounds alien to the voice that's been consistent for the 80,000 words previous.

❑ **Don't press too hard.** This is no place for breathless over-writing. Show the nice people out of your story gracefully, without losing your composure.

❑ **Above all, it's important enough to repeat, do not introduce cute endings, visual or language clichés, laborious descrip-tions, or mysterious, unresolved outcomes.** The last impres-sion you want to create is a positive one. Don't leave an audience feeling tricked or cheated.

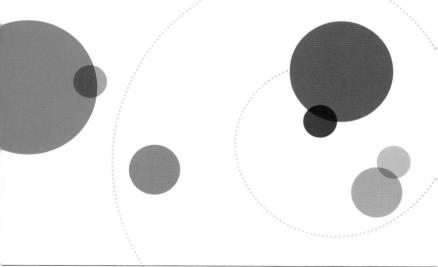

A LAST WORD ON LAST WORDS

☐ **After you've written your last word, go to work.** I've said it before: Writing is vastly overrated. You begin to craft your work into a salable, readable story and elevate yourself as a writer in revision.

☐ **Polish the ending until it dazzles.** This is the place for the best of everything you're going to market to the publishing world. You must leave your reader spent when she closes your book. The ultimate danger of damnation leads to the ultimate redemption. Edit, edit, edit until you've nothing left to give to your ending, until you, too, are spent.

☐ **Cut everything but the essential meat and bone.** Don't use obscure words. Don't write elaborately complex sentences. Don't embellish paragraphs with detours and distractions. Don't write complicated scenes with vague references or hidden meanings. Here, more than anywhere in your story is the place to be direct, active, assertive.

☐ **Trust the pacing tools and use them.** Apply the Reading Ease Ideal to every scene. Rewrite until you meet every goal in the index. Revise critical scenes until they stand higher than every other scene on the pacing scale. Whether your climax is a thousand words long or ten thousand, your reader must feel as if she's raced through it, that she cannot put down your story until it's done.

THE
end

There you go. All the best tools and helpers I own.
I wish you the best luck as you use them.
No more excuses.

BOTTOM LINE: It doesn't matter what your level of talent is as a writer, whether you're a beginner or a published pro: The Pacing Scale tool, used with the REI as a guide to editing your fiction, will make you a better writer.

> The beginning novelist will gain an edge in his work as he submits it to agents and editors. And the published pro will boost the professionalism in all her own work. Expect the level of success, no matter what that level now, to increase as you put these tools to work for you.
>
> Now. Sit. Write. Gitter done.
> See you on the best-seller lists.
>
> —JAMES V. SMITH, JR.
> JANUARY 2006

INDEX

INDEX